Besieged

RICHARD FOREMAN

© Richard Foreman 2020

Richard Foreman has asserted his rights under the Copyright, Design and Patents Act, 1988, to be identified as the author of this work.

First published in 2020 by Sharpe Books.

CONTENTS

Title	i
Chapters 1 – 21	1 – 140
Epilogue	141
End Note	145

BESIEGED

"The Lord's unfailing love and mercy still continue,
Fresh as the morning, as sure as the sunrise.
The Lord is all I have, and so I put my hope in him."
Lamentations 3: 22 – 24.

1.

Sunlight cut through the threadbare clouds, cooking combatants in their armour. Sweat stung eyes, as if pricked by needles. The tang of blood and gangrene burrowed into the air, like maggots tunnelling through corpses.

The stitches opened-up on his wound, again. Edward Kemp had contracted the injury from a crossbow quarrel slicing through his shoulder, during the sacking of Antioch. Now the English knight was in danger of suffering a similar wound - or death - from defending the walled city.

Kerbogha of Mosul had ordered yet another assault, this time on the ramparts close to the Iron Gate. The defensive line of the crusaders was spread thin, "as thin as twine" Raymond of Toulouse lamented, as Kerbogha decided to surround the city. To contain the enemy. To starve the westerners into submission. Every now and then he would launch a probing attack to bloody the enemy. Death by a thousand cuts.

The alarm had been sounded. Edward was commanding a small force of a dozen or so men on the adjoining section of the wall. He ordered the men-at-arms and a handful of archers to follow him. He felt like a firefighter, endeavouring to prevent a blaze from spreading and consuming a whole town. The Turks couldn't be allowed to take control of the walls, and then the towers – and then open the Iron Gate for the rest of the army to stream through and slaughter the Christians. As the pilgrim army had recently poured through the gates and butchered the Antiochenes – soldiers and innocent civilians alike.

Scores of enemy arrows clattered against the stone walls, like hailstones in a storm, providing covering fire. Godfrey of Bouillon and his Lotharingian knights kept their heads down, and raised their shields, to prevent being hit as they advanced towards the enemy on the far side to which Edward approached the besieging troops.

The Englishman was part of Bohemond of Taranto's company. A seasoned soldier, Edward had taken the cross to earn his fortune, rather than earn his salvation and any remission of sins.

"I used to think that I would be willing to sell my soul for a suckling pig," he had remarked to his friend and fellow knight, Hugh of Cerisy, a month ago. "Now, I'm so bloody starving, I would sell my soul for a mere pig's trotter."

Godfrey of Bouillon may have been fighting to reach Jerusalem and liberate the Holy Sepulchre - to write his name in the annals of history. But Edward was just fighting to stay alive one more day, to help preserve the life of the man fighting next to him – and to get back to Emma. To spend one more night with the woman who had worked her way into his bed and heart. Not that he could muster the strength to make love to her tonight. His whole body ached, like a giant sprain.

Edward's features hardened, clenching like a fist, as he closed upon his foes. His leather jerkin, worn over his mail shirt, was crusted with blood and dust. The knight had never lacked courage. He just hoped he wasn't lacking in luck either. Every soldier needs to pray to Fortuna as well as God. The veteran soldier forgot about his growling stomach and weakened frame. His unflinching eyes surveyed the scene. The Turkish forces had scaled a trio of ladders. They were clambering over the top of the walls like spiders. Godfrey and his knights were already engaging the enemy. They were neither advancing nor retreating. Just fighting for their lives – and the lives of every other pilgrim. Holding the line. Hacking away or thrusting their weapons forward. The sound of shields clanged against scimitars and spear points. Screams pierced the humid air, as both Christians and infidels fell - whether slashed or skewered by gore-stained blades. A Lotharingian dropped from the ramparts and landed on the street below with a sickening crack and thud. His polished armour gleamed in the afternoon sun as he gracelessly tumbled through the air and his neck snapped like a twig.

The wave of Turkish arrows ceased, either from exhausting their supply, or the bowmen were worried about hitting their comrades.

Blisters had formed on Edward's calloused hands from having to wield his weapon night and day over the past week. But still he gripped the hilt tighter. He ignored the stiffness in his shoulder and the pain in his buttock from another wound. He ignored the torrent of fear coursing through his veins like ice, as he gritted his teeth and channelled his fear into molten rage. All that mattered was the enemy in front of him – and how he was going to kill them.

A brawny, hook-nosed Turk swung his scimitar at the Englishman. Edward deflected the blow with his shield – and, with his opponent's torso exposed, punched the point of his sword through the Saracen's sternum, roaring and spitting out a curse as he did so. A group of men-at-arms soon supported the knight. One buried his chipped axe-head into a Turkish forehead, splitting it open like a melon.

For a time, the outcome of the skirmish hung in the balance. Weapons and limbs flailed. The hatred between the two sides burned as hot as the sun. One of the ladders snapped from the weight of troops scaling the walls, stemming the tide of reinforcements entering the fray. The crusaders gained an advantage too from Owen, an accomplished Welsh bowman, and his unit of archers firing down at the enemy from the roof of a nearby tower, situated behind Edward.

Nock. Pull. Loose.

The bowman, along with his English friend, had fought his way across Europe. He was a soldier for hire, who enjoyed singing, drinking and whoring in, almost, equal measure. His eyes were two slits and his arms bulged as Owen went about plying his trade.

Every one of the Welshman's arrows hit its mark, passing through mail and plate armour alike. Lodging into flesh. One missile zipped through the air and entered an enemy's eye socket, as his head appeared over the parapet. The soldier fell backwards, skittling over the men on the ladder beneath him.

The captain leading the besieging force bellowed out orders, attempting to rally his troops. He raised his bloody sword, crying "Allahu Akbar!" But just as the words finished spewing out of his mouth Edward barged through a couple of Turks and buried his sword point into the officer's gullet.

The enemy, starved of reinforcements, now struggled to fight on two fronts. Godfrey and his well-drilled force of Lotharingian knights steadily advanced. Edward's men were less disciplined, yet equally effective as they moved forward, whilst trying not to lose their footing on the dead and the dying. Normans had slaughtered Edward's parents, when he was a child, during the Harrying of the North. But he was now glad to have them fighting by his side. Fulk of Chartres, the brutal knight who had been first up the ladder to infiltrate Antioch, had trained the men-at-arms. The soldiers were perhaps more fearful of disappointing the knight than dying from a Turkish blade.

The dwindling numbers of besiegers were caught in a vice, or the jaws of death. There could be no retreat or surrender for the enemy on the battlements. Prayers, or pleas for mercy, were ignored as the Christians cut down anyone within reach of their weapons.

Edward exhaled. Rasping. Relieved. The knight felt the blood trickle out from his shoulder and stick to his tunic. After the change of watch he would pay a visit to Charles of Anjou, Bohemond's surgeon, and ask him to stitch him back up again for the third time.

"Your luck will run out one day, Edward," the Norman doctor warned his patient, as he re-stitched the soldier's wounds, after returning to duty far earlier than the surgeon advised.

"And there I was thinking that my luck ran out as soon as I signed-up for this fool's errand of a crusade," the knight replied, his voice rough with wine and weariness. Most people found it difficult to tell when the Englishman was being droll or sincere. Edward couldn't always tell either.

"You should rest."

"I'll rest enough when I'm dead, or when Kerbogha decides he's homesick and retreats back to Mosul."

Godfrey wiped his sword upon a Turkish corpse, as his lieutenant, Conrad, issued orders to deal with the enemy wounded.

"Finish them all off. Strip them of their weapons and any food they possess... Toss their bodies back over the walls, to serve as an example for any other bastard thinking of attacking us. If their Muslim brothers try to recover the bodies, rain arrows or rocks down upon them. The only good Turk is a dead Turk," Conrad remarked. When the Christian had taken part in the crusaders' pogroms in the Rhineland he had argued that, "the only good Jew is a dead Jew."

Tiredness was sovereign over triumphalism. There was a time when the crusaders would have celebrated such a victory and goaded the enemy. But the soldiers were war weary. They needed to save their strength, for the struggle ahead.

The prince nodded to Edward, in appreciation. Both men also offered one another a brief half-smile. But even the muscles in the corner of their mouths were weak or atrophied.

"Your reputation as a fighter precedes you, Edward. And it is well deserved. Perhaps we should have recruited more Englishmen to our cause. More of the enemy may now be slain," Godfrey remarked. His voice was clear, confident – as smooth as glass.

"Aye, but you would have run out of wine and ale much earlier, I warrant," Edward argued, half-joking. Fortunately, his countrymen were more enamoured with their taverns than the attractions of the Holy Land. Although many would be happy to be free from their wives whilst serving in the Army of God, the knight judged, as he took in the lauded prince. Godfrey, like the towering Englishman, stood taller than the men around him. He had grown slender over the past month, Edward fancied. Even a prince of Godfrey's rank could not afford to eat as he once did. Or if he could, his purse would eventually grow as narrow as his figure. "Godfrey is as handsome as he is noble. I would abandon you quicker than the Emperor deserted us, should he court me," Emma had teasingly commented to Edward. It was rumoured that Godfrey possessed a man in his retinue who trimmed his blond hair and beard every morning. The prince could trace his bloodline back to Charlemagne, which he was happy to remind people of every day too. There was little doubting Godfrey's courage and faith. His company were loyal to him and the crusader had grown in stature, as both a soldier and leader, since crossing the Bosphorus. His commitment to the cause was steadfast from the beginning. Godfrey had sold his feudal lands to help fund his army. He also generated capital by extorting money from Jewish merchants and bankers throughout his territories. More than any other prince, Godfrey still believed that the crusaders would reach and liberate Jerusalem, despite their current dire position.

"It's our destiny," Edward had overheard Godfrey assert at a meeting with the other great princes. "This may be our darkest hour. But it is always darkest before the dawn. As you know, I experienced a vision. I was standing before the city of Jerusalem, with our banner flying over St Stephen's Gate. A cross once again hung within the Holy Sepulchre. God's heavenly light poured down across the city. Clouds opened up, like an angel's wings... 'Tis just a dream, you may argue. But it is a dream we should still believe in."

But the Englishman's dreams diverged from the Christian prince's ambition. England, not Jerusalem, was home. It had been an age since he had witnessed a lush, green landscape or fished in a secluded stream. He missed singing songs in his native language, frothy beers and jokes that would make a bawd blush. Edward resolved to live with Emma in a quiet village, away from depraved clergymen and a rapacious Norman baron, who would tax you quicker than a banker would lend you money. He was even looking forward to enduring his country's sodden climate and bland cuisine. The soldier was tired of waking up to an unforgiving sun, bone dry landscapes and the stench of putrefying flesh. But, ironically, every step closer to Jerusalem could be considered a step closer to England. The only way back west was to continue east – to finish what they started. Edward realised he even missed London a little, populated by odious lawyers and merchants wearing the latest fashions – and thinking everyone else backwards. London was also home to less sartorial rogues who would steal the teeth from a corpse's mouth. More than one tavern goer would slit another's throat over a spilled drink or ill-judged cuss. But still Edward yearned to become a regular of such an alehouse again, with mead, straw and blood strewn across the floor. He had courted his first barmaid in such an establishment (it had cost him the price of a jug of wine - and the courtship and consummation of the relationship, behind the outhouse, had taken all of an hour or two). He had broken his first nose in a tavern brawl. His victim had been an arrogant Norman squire. The Englishman fractured his hand as a result of the blow. But it had been worth it.

Edward wondered if William Rufus was still on the throne. Rufus was the son of William the Conqueror or, as many Englishmen called him, William the Bastard. But he wasn't the only bastard in the realm, the knight fancied. There were greedy bastards, vicious bastards, drunken bastards and pious bastards. *We're all bastards in some way.*

Home is where the heart is. But, even more than England, his heart belonged to Emma. When he finally learned to pray again, he had asked God to keep her safe. Edward sometimes imagined returning to the country of his birth, accompanied by the madam. No one knew her there. She wouldn't be judged a sinner or outcast. They could make a fresh start. He dared to hope, but then chided himself for doing so. Hope may cost nothing, but it should be treated like a scarce commodity and used sparingly.

Godfrey was not immune to hope too, in relation to recruiting the English knight.

"If ever you find yourself in need of a company, after serving Bohemond, you will find a home here. I intend to reach Jerusalem. God may have a plan for you too, Edward," the Christian prince proffered.

"If God somehow does have a plan for me, I'd be more than happy for Him to bestow it upon someone else," the knight drolly replied, neither accepting or spurning Godfrey's proposal.

I'd rather go back to England as a living coward, than a dead hero.

2.

Bohemond of Taranto had installed himself in the former residence of Yaghi Siyan. He wanted to give the impression he was the new governor. Or king. The Norman commander had been the first to enter the city and raise his banner. Therefore, according to the law of conquest, Antioch belonged to him. But the prince's rival, Raymond of Toulouse, argued that the law of conquest was redundant, in light of the oaths they had given to the Emperor, to cede the city to him. Their dispute would have to be resolved after they survived the siege. If they survived the siege.

The property had seen better days. Any valuables not taken by Siyan and his retinue were looted by the crusaders, during the sacking. The governor managed to escape from the city, but then fell from his horse and was murdered by an Armenian butcher. His head was hacked off and presented to the crusaders. The food stores in the house were raided and stripped clean like vultures devouring a corpse. Blood still stained rugs and carpets. Bannisters were broken. Walls and ceilings were charred. The acrid smell of smoke still infused the upholstery. The house was as decrepit, creaking, as a crippled elder, Thomas Devin thought to himself, as the scribe waited for Bohemond in the dining room. The chamber was one of those being restored to its former glory. The floor had been scrubbed clean of gore, although Thomas thought he could still view pieces of chipped bone on the ground. The smell of smoke had been ousted by incense and the aroma of freshly baked bread. Bohemond had "borrowed" pieces of furniture from other properties to equip his own. Tapestries and paintings, depicting either battles or scenes from the gospels, decorated the walls, along with ornate candlesticks. Whereas other leading crusaders prominently hung a crucifix in their dining areas, for their guests to see, a large broad sword served as a cross in the chamber, behind where Bohemond sat.

In the background Thomas could hear hammering. Wooden shutters were being repaired and replaced at the front on the house. Bohemond had recently acquired a polished bronze flagpole, which he hoisted his standard upon. As much as most of the inside of the residence was in a state of disrepair the prince was mindful of projecting an outward show of authority – and majesty.

Thomas' stomach groaned. It was likely someone in the next room, or building, could hear it, he fancied. As enervated as the young Englishman felt he still gripped his knife and fork tightly, anticipating the promised meal. Thomas used to feel guilty about eating well at Bohemond's table, whilst the majority of his fellow pilgrims, women and children, would be starving. He often secreted food about his person and passed it on to the less fortunate. But, although he still felt guilty, his body ordered his mind to devour any food like a ravenous wolf. Few now knew where their next meal was coming from. Table manners – and Christian fellowship – were not as they once were.

The scholar, after visiting the famed monastery at Cluny, had heard Pope Urban II preach his epochal sermon at Clermont. The pontiff had called upon Christians, or more particularly Christian knights, to take up the cross and arrange an armed pilgrimage to the East, to liberate Jerusalem and defeat the murderous infidels. Thomas' father, a wealthy wool merchant, paid Bohemond to take his son into his company. Although a non-combatant, the young Englishman had proved invaluable to the Norman prince as a clerk and translator. "You pick up languages quicker than some of my men pick up the pox," Bohemond had once exclaimed.

Thomas' build was slight, even before the shortage of provisions began to bite. His face had lost its puppy fat and innocence. His drained countenance was leaner, harder. The pilgrim who was sitting at Bohemond's table, was not the same pilgrim who had set off, after having a final meal with his family. The lustre in his aspect had dulled, like a gem cloudy with grime. Curiosity had turned into cynicism. A sense of wonder had turned into a sense of weariness. During the sacking of Antioch, the devout Christian had committed a mortal sin. He had killed a man, Girard of Mortain, in order to save his friend and countryman, Edward Kemp. There was blood, real and metaphorical, on his hands. The sin, as much as starvation, was eating away at him, Thomas believed. There could be no absolution. He was too ashamed – and frightened – to tell Bishop Adhemar, for fear that the clergyman would look at him differently. Thomas had not been the same since the incident. Yet, as dreadful as the act was, he reasoned that he would do it again.

"Rather him than us," Edward had argued, after sensing how traumatised his friend was.

"What I did was a sin," Thomas replied, with a faraway look in his eyes – perhaps wishing he could be faraway, back home, himself.

"You killed a man. God knows you will have to kill some more before you reach Jerusalem. Or you will never reach Jerusalem. In case you haven't noticed, there are a fair few thousand Turks and Arabs standing between here and your holy shrines and relics. And they want to slay you, far more than you want to slay them. This pilgrimage was always going to be a bloody affair. The angels were never going to carry us to Jerusalem on their wings. We are all sinners. At least you know what you did was a sin. The first sin is the denial of sin. God help me, I'm even starting to quote the scriptures now," the knight remarked, surprising himself. To help him learn his letters, Edward had taken to reading passages of the books which Adhemar kept in his private chambers, when the two men shared a jug of wine together.

"I could be damned," Thomas argued, his expression as troubled as his soul.

Edward let out a burst of full-throated laughter.

"Take heart that you won't be alone in Hell. God knows, we're all damned," the knight replied. Although he considered that if any of his fellow crusaders were worthy of a place in Heaven, Thomas would be as good a candidate as any.

Yet the translator's soul was still to be shriven. He seldom slept, despite his fatigue. He ceased reading and composing poetry - and the Bible no longer provided the consolation it once did. He replayed the act of his mortal sin, both in his nightmares and waking thoughts. Thomas had swapped his sword over, to get rid of the murder weapon. But he was unable to swap out his feelings, to scrub out the stain on his conscience the way that Bohemond had scrubbed out the blood on the floor.

Thomas heard his host's footsteps, before he entered the chamber. Along with his new billet, the Norman prince had seen better days, Thomas judged. His beard had not been trimmed for at least a week. His short blond hair had grown lank and long. His blue eyes were rimmed with sleeplessness, but they could still both charm and chill alike. The young Englishman was not the only pilgrim to note how the commander sometimes now walked with his head hanging down. Downcast. Defeated. But his mask of command seldom slipped. For the most part his features still projected a sense of strength and determination. Bohemond of Taranto had the weight of the world on his shoulders, but still he stood over half a hand taller than the likes of Godfrey and Edward. Bohemond had been named after a legendary giant. Now people would name their children after the legendary soldier.

The famed, or infamous, prince was still clad in his expensive, but well used, armour. The chest plate was riddled with dints and blood stains. As with all other pilgrims Bohemond had lost weight, but it only served to accentuate his muscular frame. His chest was as broad as any archer's, his powerful arms and legs resembled a wrestler. "Bohemond was made for war – and war made him," Adhemar had once remarked to Thomas. As well as seeming a tower of strength, Bohemond – the son of Robert Guiscard – was also renowned for his guile and tactical genius. "He is constant in his inconstancy. Bohemond is only loyal to one person. Bohemond," Thomas had overheard Raymond of Toulouse exclaim. The Norman prince had campaigned against his own brother over the years. His former enemy, the Byzantine emperor, was now an erstwhile ally – albeit the crusader was willing break his oath to Alexios and keep Antioch as his own prize. His ally would become an enemy once more. Whilst many of the crusader princes eyed Jerusalem as their ultimate goal, Bohemond was ever mindful of the greater prize of Constantinople. He was determined to end the war his father began. Betraying Alexios would come as easily to him as a blacksmith shoeing a horse.

Although there were some who doubted Bohemond's character, few doubted his military prowess, courage and leadership. When he spoke, people listened. He had recently been the saviour of the campaign. Bohemond had worked with an Armenian, Firuz, to gain access to the city and open its gates – breaking the siege before Kerbogha's relief army arrived. Without the Norman prince, the campaign would be over. Few had bloodied their sword more too, as Bohemond fought on the frontline to prevent the Turks from descending on the city via the citadel. He bolstered the defences – and his soldiers' courage. Much to Raymond of Toulouse's chagrin, who once deemed himself the chief commander of the Army of God, the pilgrims now looked to Bohemond to save them again. To work another miracle.

The commander had just come from calling upon some of his troops, standing a watch near the Iron Gate. He had brought them a small measure of wine and tried to raise their spirits by discussing past triumphs. As well as the surrounding Muslim army, baying for their blood, boredom and starvation were their enemies. Growls of hunger out-sounded any bursts of laughter. Bohemond knew only too well how it was a soldier's lot to wait. To wait to fight. To wait to eat. To wait to sleep. To help distract them, after he left, Bohemond ordered his men to sharpen their weapons as they kept watch. A blade could never be too sharp.

"Food," the magnate barked, as he slumped into a chair at the head of the large, cedarwood table in the middle of the room. For a moment Thomas worried that the chair, with its legs bowing slightly, might collapse under the weight the prince's frame, armour and sins. The table was sturdy and well crafted, with ornate scroll work along the sides, but the nobleman was critical of the piece of furniture for being smaller than Raymond of Toulouse's main dining table.

A scrawny attendant appeared at the door, nodded his head and then disappeared again, to fetch some bread and cheese from the kitchen.

Bohemond took in the nervous looking scribe. Thomas owned a love of learning and God, but he seemed to care for little else. He had come a long way, in more ways than one, however, Bohemond judged. Few knew it, but the entire pilgrimage was in the young Englishman's debt. The translator had been instrumental in liaising with Firuz's agent, so they could infiltrate Antioch and sack the city. Thomas was more intelligent – and braver – than many in his company gave him credit for.

The prince hadn't seen Thomas in over a week, but he had visibly changed. Starvation had eaten away at him. But that was to be expected. His cheekbones were as sharp as the sword he wore. His ribcage would doubtless be pronounced, should Thomas lift-up his tunic. A strong gust of wind could probably blow him over, Bohemond fancied, such was his enfeebled state. A vacancy had replaced his bright, engaged aspect. His expression was often pained, rather than pensive. Thomas offered up a polite rather than joyful smile. But what had he, or anyone else, had cause to be joyful about?

Bohemond didn't smile back, either too fatigued or despondent to do so.

"How is your Arabic progressing?" the prince asked, without any preamble. The day after the sacking of Antioch, Bohemond had ordered the translator to improve his fluency in their enemy's tongue. He had even arranged for a native of the city to tutor the student. "I neither want you to be modest or boastful. Honesty is the best policy," the secretive and duplicitous commander remarked.

"My Arabic is now sufficient for me to carry out conversations. I have been visiting Omer every morning," the gifted linguist replied.

"Excellent. My intention is not to have you speak the language, but to ensure that you are conversant enough to understand others. I once called upon you before, Thomas, to help save the crusade. I am hoping that lightning will strike twice in the same place. I am forming a plan. We cannot just wait around to starve and die. Muslims are not renowned for their Christian mercy. We're either going to have to kill them, or they are going to kill us. My preference is for the former. Desperate times call for desperate measures. I believe that the quote comes from Hippocrates, no? I am not without a little learning. But a little learning will suffice," Bohemond remarked. The prince smiled, He had a sly sense of humour, as well as a sly temperament, Thomas considered. Few could tell what was going on behind his mask of command. "Kerbogha has made me desperate. I am hoping that he lives to regret doing so." The soldier here gripped the hilt of his sword so tightly that Thomas imagined he might snap it off. "I have faith in you, that you will be equal to the task I will shortly set you."

The diffident Englishman offered up another polite smile. Thomas was pleased that the prince had faith in him. He just wasn't sure if he had faith in himself. Or God.

3.

The bishop's knees cracked – and he nearly stumbled when rising to his feet – after praying. Dusk, glowing like embers, coloured the sky through the window, which also afforded a view of the Church of St Peter. The building seemed to be crumbling before his very eyes. Twilight bestowed a blessed, if brief, cooling breeze. A dirty, infernal heat plagued the days. The chill wind could slice through one's skin, like a blade, at night. Adhemar wistfully, or wearily, wondered if his act of praying was borne from habit, belief or desperation. As with most issues, the answer involved a mix of things, he judged. His aristocratic features were creased in anxiety. He couldn't remember the last time he had slept all the way through the night. Crows' feet perched on the corners of his intelligent and kind eyes.

Although he could not claim to feel inspired, or inspirational, at present none would contest that Adhemar was the spiritual leader of the crusade (despite the popularity of the firebrand preacher, Peter the Hermit, who possessed a zealous following among many of the non-combatant pilgrims). Adhemar had been the first to kneel before Pope Urban at Clermont and take the cross. The bishop had also proved invaluable due to his skills as a diplomat. Not only did he forge a strong friendship with Tatikios, the Emperor's envoy, but without Adhemar's calm and conciliatory temper the purpose and unity between the Frank and Norman princes would have faltered. Both Raymond of Toulouse and Bohemond of Taranto respected Adhemar. It was one of the only things they could agree on. The aristocrat, who possessed the common touch, was not devoid of physical courage and martial virtues too. Edward had first encountered the mild-mannered bishop in the heat of battle, at Dorylaeum. Without the clergyman's abilities as a logistician, the pilgrimage would not have endured on the plains of Antioch for over six months. But it was beyond even the authority and talents of the man of

God to prevent the end of the campaign, now they were inside the city.

Adhemar sat at his desk and picked up his stylus, to continue to write to his friend and confessor, William of Falaise. It was doubtful if his letter would ever reach his old companion, but he still felt compelled to share his thoughts – as he also felt compelled to pray, not knowing if his pleas were reaching God. If only problems shared were problems halved. Adhemar had regularly corresponded with William over the years. They would discuss the works of Aristotle and St Augustine – and gossip about fellow clergyman with their - to say the least – minor foibles. But now the bishop felt like Jeremiah, when writing to his friend. His letters were a litany of misfortunes, befalling the crusade. Adhemar had spent most of the day composing various missives. He had written to Urban and Alexios, framing their parlous fate and asking, if not indeed begging, for assistance. The bishop had even written to Baldwin, a crusader prince, the brother of Godfrey of Bouillon, who had deserted the main campaign to further his personal ambitions and rule Edessa. But Baldwin could make even Bohemond appear selfless, Adhemar realised. There was more chance of Agamemnon or Caesar returning from the grave to come to their aid. But "where there's life, there's hope", Adhemar mused, quoting Cicero. Hopefully his messenger could, through guile or bribery, slip through Kerbogha's cordon. The bishop had been candid with Urban, Alexios and Baldwin – in relation to the immediate peril the pilgrims faced. But with his old friend, Adhemar felt he could be even more frank - and bare his shredded soul.

"...I used to believe that God was testing us. Now he may be punishing us. I used to envision our pilgrimage as an act of charity, as well as liberation. I believed that we could bestow the torch of civilisation – shine a light in the darkness – in relation to the East. I thought we could convert a portion of the people we encountered. But the road to Hell is paved with good intentions. An English knight put it bluntly to me recently, that our mission is an act of conquest, not charity.

Not even all the clergy at the Vatican and Cluny could pray away our sins, given the atrocities in the Rhineland.

We can but pay for our sins. We are penned in, like mangy sheep, waiting to be slaughtered. My last letter recounted our victory, in recovering Antioch (if indeed we can deem such a barbaric action a triumph). But it was a Pyrrhic victory, at best. The besiegers became the besieged, within a few short days. If the Four Horsemen of the Apocalypse had appeared on the horizon, approaching the Iron Bridge, our people would have been less afeared.

Kerbogha has mobilised an army over three times our size. He first engaged a fortress we constructed outside the city whilst we assaulted Antioch. Robert of Flanders and his company fought bravely, but in vain, to hold La Mahomerie. Ultimately Robert and his dwindling force had to retreat at night, setting fire to the structure so our fortress couldn't be used against as. As the flames licked the air it signalled the beginning of a season in hell. Kerbogha next turned his attention to taking command of the citadel, embedded in the mountain like a stone lodged in a boot, perched over the city. If we could have somehow secured the stronghold, we would now be more confident of securing the city. The citadel is a gateway to the outside, but conversely it is also an entrance into the city. Bohemond knew only too well the strategic value of the stronghold, which is why he attempted to capture it as soon as he entered the city. Although Yaghi Siyan abandoned his post, quicker than a king may take a mistress after marriage, his son, Shams ad-Daulah, was more courageous and cannier. He won the race, on the night of the sacking, to fortify the citadel. But, either by force or bribery, Kerbogha took possession of the asset. He immediately mobilised a force on the slopes of Mount Silphius. A horde. They poured down the mountain like lava, attempting to destroy anything in their wake, funnelling towards an opening which enjoined a road leading to the city. But our men dammed up the opening, through a wall of iron, flesh and stone. The infidels hammered upon the door, but we didn't let them in. I understand that Kerbogha is a keen chess player – and he sacrificed his men like pawns, as they martyred themselves on the points of our spears and swords. The fighting was vicious and relentless. Day after day, night after night, there was a clash of arms. Screams constantly curdled the air. As much as I was advised not to, I could not countenance abandoning the fight and my fellow pilgrims. I drew my sword too. There was not a visage free from blood and bruises. I allowed one of our churches to be used as a temporary hospital, but it resembled a charnel house. Bohemond was a tower of strength, the difference between survival or surrender, as he personally fought in the shield wall. His knights and men-at-arms often lost their footing on the pools of blood and corpses beneath their feet. I'm not sure if the prince was inspired by his obstinacy, his faith in God or self-preservation. Bohemond wasn't the only nobleman to show his mettle. At one point he advanced so far forward that Robert of Flanders and Robert of Normandy had to cut a furrow through the enemy too and save the commander. Tancred and Godfrey have also come of age. I was recently told of how one knight, aptly named Mad Hugh, singlehandedly defended a tower against a band of Turkish fighters. He broke three spears during the frenzied melee. If any poets or chroniclers survive this siege, they will immortalise their deeds.

But I fear our heroes will ultimately be deemed tragic heroes. We dared to take the fight to the enemy the other day. Whilst Kerbogha decided to choke us by surrounding the city - instead of lancing us, through advancing via the citadel – we launched a breakout attack against one of their camps through a postern gate in our walls. The Turks were surprised – and routed. I watched the action from the battlements. I dared to hope, that we could secure sufficient provisions – and that our soldiers would return safely. But Kerbogha was quick in ordering a counterattack – and too many of our troops were caught looting the camp. We retreated. But we were exposed, like deer left vulnerable in a field, and became the victim of Turkish arrows and spear points. Many of our soldiers were trampled to death, as they tried to re-enter the city through the narrow postern gate. It was like trying to force a loaf of bread through a keyhole. Victory turned to defeat. A massacre. A father of one of the soldiers involved in the attack was standing beside me, as the slaughter unfolded. He howled in grief and bloodied and broke his hand, as he repeatedly punched a wall and cursed the Muslims – and his own God. St Peter himself would not have been able to provide the man with any consolation to placate his soul, so I did not even try. He was as wizened and piteous as Job.

We can no longer consider if we will triumph, but rather when we will fail. Disease and defeatism are spreading through the city like a virulent plague. Even Raymond of Toulouse hasn't proved immune to the malady. His knights perform admirably in their duties, but my old friend no longer seems to have the stomach for the fight. There may be an element of petulance in his pessimism, however. The crusade no longer looks to the count to take the lead. Doubly insulting for him, they look to his rival, Bohemond, to assume command. "All is lost," Raymond pronounced the other day. "It is not a matter of if Kerbogha breaks us. But when." It was telling that no one had the spirit or argument to counter this view.

Still we pray. Some pray for God to deliver us, some pray for Emperor Alexios to arrive with a relief force. Doubts and despair proliferate like cinders swirling off a funeral pyre. More than a few of my congregants have started to faint during mass – and not because they are overawed by my sermons. Starvation is as rife as despair. Indeed, the former is inspiring the latter. I tried my best to manage what little remained of the city's food stores after the sacking, distributing provisions fairly and making any rations last. But my best wasn't good enough. Starvation can ravage a man, strip him of his dignity. I recalled a passage from Corinthians the other day. "Food, however, will not improve our relations with God; we shall not lose anything if we do not eat, nor shall we gain anything if we do eat." I couldn't help but doubt the verisimilitude of the scriptures. People feel like they are being disembowelled every day. Hunger feeds lassitude, irritability and desperation. Good Christians turn on each other over a piece of mouldy cheese. Veins are being cut on animals – and blood imbibed like wine. We need more than just spiritual nourishment. Even the princes now eat like peasants – and the peasants eat like savages. Horse flesh is a delicacy. Vines and thistles – even pieces of putrefied leather – are boiled down and called "a stew". Some have even taken to eating their own shoes. Pilgrims eat nettles, bark and other strange plants which they know will make them ill, or even cause them to die – but still they devour them like wretched beasts. Perhaps people thought they were endowed with riches, after looting Antioch. But again, are we not paying for our sins? A loaf of bread presently costs a whole bezant. I heard that Duke Godfrey paid fifteen marks of silver for the rancid hide of a camel. If only our morale could increase at the pace of the rising price of food. We need a miracle, akin to Christ feeding the five thousand, if we are to survive the month. Although, in some ways, I consider it a miracle that we have held out for this long. But surrender equates to death. We cannot let the enemy decide our fate or abduct our women and children."

Adhemar flexed his hand, as he felt it cramping up. He was tired. Tired of everything. *We need a miracle*, he thought to himself, as the sound of a sigh accompanied the noise of his rumbling stomach. *But I am not so sure that we are deserving of one.*

The bishop considered whether he should close his letter with some sentiments, pertaining to how much William's friendship meant to him. It was likely to be his last letter to his fellow priest. But, if he somehow conceded this, he would be conceding defeat.

My faith may have diminished. But it hasn't vanished completely.

Adhemar was distracted from his thoughts by a gentle knock on the door.

"Enter."

His clerk, Rainald, appeared. Gaunt. As thin as a shin bone.

"Your guests have arrived," the Frank announced, his voice hoarser than normal.

"Thank you, Rainald."

Adhemar had arranged to meet Raymond of Toulouse. The prince sent a message earlier, asking if he could introduce the bishop to someone.

Peter Bartholomew.

4.

Flames upon candles flickered – wriggling – as a slight draught wafted into the room at their entrance. Raymond wore a fine, purple surcoat embroidered with silken and golden thread. His coat of arms was emblazoned on his left breast. His iron-grey hair and beard had been freshly trimmed. A strong jaw, along with a stolid frame, projected an air of strength and authority. Although he was no longer in his prime – the past year had aged him considerably – Adhemar fancied that he wouldn't envy any Turk who confronted Raymond on the battlefield.

Adhemar offered the prince an appreciative nod and cordial smile. The bishop was pleased to see the count – and pleased to see him reciprocate his greeting. There had recently been some bad blood between the two old friends. Raymond felt spurned and betrayed when Adhemar sided with his bitter rival, Bohemond – and supported the Norman's plan to attack and capture the city. Adhemar had to endorse the plan, as it was the only plan they had. The clergyman regretted that Raymond felt that he had switched his allegiance to Bohemond. He hoped for a détente with nobleman – and not just because Raymond possessed the greatest army and treasury among the princes.

In behind Raymond walked a rake-thin peasant, Peter Bartholomew, wearing a tunic made of a material which was little better than sackcloth. Around his neck, the pilgrim wore a cross, which couldn't exactly be deemed a subtle size. He was a young man, but privation and the rigours of the campaign had taken its toll. A mop of auburn hair was marked with grey, dried blood and grime. His fringe covered an old wound, from where Bartholomew had been fighting on the slopes of Mount Silphius. His fingernails were as black as tar, yet still he chewed them a few times throughout his interview with the clergyman. A broken nose and twisted mouth dominated his round face. Either he possessed a squint, or there was a slight furtive element to his expression, Adhemar judged as he took in his guest. Bartholomew reminded the bishop of an unrepentant thief, who he had apprehended in his church, during an attempt to steal a silver plate and chalice after an evening mass.

"This is Peter Bartholomew, a special young man," Raymond asserted, placing a paternal hand on his companion's shoulder. "I believe that God is speaking through him. We should listen."

"Did you lose many more men today?" Emma asked Edward, as they lay in bed, beneath their fur quilt. Her body was slotted next to his, their limbs entwined, as if neither wanted to let the other go. They had been too tired to make love, but they were content just to embrace one another, to feel skin on skin.

"Aye. Most to disease and starvation," Edward replied, his voice a sigh, his expression haunted, as he pictured the emaciated bodies of friends and brothers-in-arms. Some died with a sense of relief or deliverance, as if gently drifting off to sleep. Some died in agony, drenched in sweat and calling for loved ones. "A soldier shouldn't perish in such a way. No one should."

The knight thought how their forces once stood as mighty as an oak. Kerbogha had recently tried to take an axe to the Army of God – and chop it down in one mighty stroke by an all-out assault via the citadel. But now the enemy were using a thousand small blades to whittle away the crusade, into nothing.

Their room stood on the top floor of one of the largest houses in the centre of the city. Bohemond had assigned the property to the madam – and Emma had duly turned the building into a brothel. She had partitioned numerous rooms, using blankets, to create more space for her girls to service their customers. The kitchen and dining area on the ground floor had been reworked into a reception room and makeshift tavern.

An empty bowl, previously containing goat stew and some crusty bread, sat on a table next to the bed. Even before they entered Antioch, the madam had instructed her girls to accept gifts and payments of food in exchange for their time. Edward had recently joked how, "We're living like kings, or at least now eating like princes." Emma could be a hard-headed businesswoman, but she was also kind-hearted and cared for the welfare of her girls – and not just because they produced revenue for her, as if she were a farmer looking after livestock. The madam had become a rich woman during the campaign.

"I hope you're not just with me for my money," Emma had joked earlier in the evening.

"No, I'm far fonder of you because of your other assets," Edward countered, with a leer, as he kissed her breasts.

Emma was wearing the last of the perfume which Edward liked. She briefly closed her eyes and took in the bouquet of the wine they were drinking and the sound of the purring fire, imagining she was back in her chambers in Taranto. Yet she realised that she would rather be with Edward, in the city of the damned, than alone in southern Italy.

Similarly, despite being surrounded by thousands of foes, who were more than keen to slit his throat or eviscerate the knight, Edward strangely felt safe and at peace whilst in her arms.

The couple had met several months ago. Lust developed into friendship – and then love. They made each other laugh, creating an island of joy in a sea of misery. He made her feel younger – cherished. She did not have to play a part when with him. Emma had stopped seeing customers since they had moved into the house in Antioch. Edward never told her to cease working, or tried to possess her, unlike other suitors in the past, which is why she chose to be faithful to him. To belong to the Englishman. He was similarly devoted to her. He loved waking up in the morning to the Italian beauty. When he came home from a day's fighting, she would bathe his body and wash the blood out of his hair, without comment or judgement. There were times, when the sun poured through the window at dawn, when her skin glowed. Emma was proof of God's existence. She was worth praying for.

Worth dying for.

Raymond introduced Bartholomew, explaining that he was a servant of William Peyre of Cunhlat. The magnate had heard rumours, back before entering Antioch, of there being a visionary in his camp. The visionary was a gifted preacher too – and was brought to the prince's attention by a number of knights, as well as commoners.

"...Peter has fought for our cause. He volunteered to participate in perilous foraging parties – and has not shirked his duties in fighting on the walls and on the slopes of Mount Silphius... Peter will be the first to confess that he has not led a blameless life, but I can testify to the quality of his character. One of my priests, Stephen of Valence, has also interviewed Peter and believes him to be a good Christian... If Peter's vision proves false, then we will lose nothing. But should it prove true, then we will gain everything. Disbelief will turn into ardent faith... But I will here let Peter speak for himself."

Raymond's voice was full of enthusiasm and conviction. Adhemar suspected the prince had rehearsed his lines. The bishop recognised a similar fervent gleam in his eye to when his old friend had taken possession of a chalice, once belonging to St Robert of Chaise-Dieu - and when he claimed to have secured one of Charlemagne's swords. Whilst Raymond spoke Adhemar occasionally glanced at his other guest, whose gaze darted around the room. The clergyman uncharitably believed that Bartholomew was calculating what he would steal, if his host turned his back on him for a moment. Before speaking he straightened his hair and adjusted his tunic, as if he were about to introduce himself to the parents of a wench he was courting.

"I used to believe I was cursed, but I may be blessed," Bartholomew announced. Any furtiveness in his countenance vanished. The pilgrim bowed to the bishop before speaking – and appeared to be a picture of solemnity. The lay preacher also sanded off the rough edges to his voice. "I tried to just dismiss my first visitation. I told myself it was the wine. But I couldn't ignore my second vision and the ones which followed."

"Who visited you, may I ask?" Adhemar remarked, half-expecting how his guest would answer.

"Our Lord Jesus Christ. And St Andrew. I still hear their voices in my waking hours, as well as see them in my dreams. Whether travelling through Mamistra or Edessa, during my foraging missions, the visions followed me. St Andrew explained how Christ had been stabbed by a Roman soldier, called Longinus, during his crucifixion. He was impaled by a lance – the Holy Lance. When I was in the desert, the apostle pointed in the direction of Antioch, saying that I should find and recover the sacred relic, which had been consecrated with Christ's own blood. When we entered the city, St Andrew then pointed to the Church of St Peter, revealing that the relic was buried beneath the floor of the basilica."

As Bartholomew delivered his account, he raised his arm and pointed - imitating the figure from his alleged vision. Adhemar noted how the direction of his pointing was opposite to the location of the Church of St Peter, however.

"I was told to be a messenger. At first, I was frightened. I pleaded with the saint to choose someone else to deliver his message, someone worthier. I have not always been a good Christian. But he replied that I would be redeeming my past sins by following his instruction. I was once a slave to grosser pleasures. I was a wretch, before I experienced God's love and mercy. If I can be saved, then everyone can…Yet still I did not immediately share my vision. I thought I might be mocked or punished. But I needed to do my duty, to God and my fellow pilgrims. I must share what the holy saint – he had red hair and a thick white beard, black eyes and an agreeable countenance – revealed to me. That once Antioch fell, I was to implore pilgrims - princes and paupers - to recover the Holy Lance, so it could be used as a standard. "He that carries this lance in battle shall never be overcome by the enemy," St Andrew proclaimed. You must allow me to complete my mission and excavate the relic. I beg you. Only then will I find peace – and the crusade be delivered," Bartholomew remarked, raising his eyes up to heaven, with a semblance of a beatific expression plastered on his roguish face.

Inside, Adhemar grimaced, winced and raised more than one sceptical eyebrow, as the peasant vindicated himself and his assumed vision. Dreams and visions were commonplace. Indeed, the bishop had once half-joked that, such were their ubiquity, it was the people who didn't claim to have experienced them who were special. Adhemar had also lost count of the number of dedicated Christians, or devout charlatans, who had tried to sell him relics over the years. He had been offered enough pieces of the True Cross to form a forest. A seamstress had claimed ownership of a shawl, once belonging to Mary Magdalene. When Adhemar questioned how new the shawl looked, the woman replied that "it was part of the miracle". William had also written to his friend once, describing how one of his congregants visited him and pulled out a severed toe, proclaiming it was once attached to the foot of St Paul. His fellow bishop mentioned how the peasant walked in and out of his chambers with a subtle limp.

Yet Adhemar needed to consider giving the benefit of the doubt to the peasant, for the sake of avoiding a slight against Raymond. It surely couldn't do any harm to indulge his old friend, he reasoned. They were more likely to find a unicorn head than the Holy Lance, particularly as the bishop knew that the relic was already in the possession of Alexios in Constantinople. Should he try and forbid the prince from retrieving the artefact then Raymond might defy him and enter the basilica regardless of his protests. The magnate was not accustomed to hearing the word "no".

"I am not here to ask you to wholeheartedly believe in Peter, but you must at least grant the opportunity to prove him right or wrong – and allow us to excavate the site. It is not just my desire to find the Holy Lance and use it as our standard. Many pilgrims have heard word of Peter's visions. If you deny them then you are more likely to fuel the fire in their bellies, rather than quench it."

Despite the hint of a threat, Raymond's tone was measured and accompanied by a supplicatory look. But Adhemar knew how the count's expression could harden like cement – and his request could turn into a demand in the blink of an eye. The bishop decided to assent to Raymond's proposal. The gesture would hopefully serve to reconcile himself to his old friend and heal any rift. He also did not want to dampen the warrior's new-found spirit and extinguish the light in his eyes, like pinching out the candles after a service.

Adhemar assured Raymond that they would begin to excavate the site the following morning.

Let us hope that the hole does not become a grave, to bury my reputation in, the bishop thought to himself.

5.

Word spread, like typhoid, through the city in the morning. Bishop Adhemar believed in Peter Bartholomew and his divine vision, many pilgrims asserted. The floor of the church would be dug up. They would find the Holy Lance and defeat their enemies. Raymond of Toulouse mobilised a number of his soldiers to pass on the news. The people began to congregate outside the Church of St Peter. Knights, clergymen and peasants populated the throng. Women brought their ruddy-faced children along.

Adhemar was surprised – and a little worried – by the size of the crowd when he arrived at the church. He had perhaps underestimated the potency of the vision and need for hope. The bishop was accompanied by Raymond and Peter Bartholomew. The latter had changed into fresh garments, provided by the count. He now resembled a monk. The bishop took in the expectant gathering. Many stood open-mouthed with wonder. Some crossed themselves or clutched crucifixes around their neck. Others clutched their bellies, suffering from hunger pangs. Adhemar noticed Peter the Hermit lingering in the background, poking his head over the crowd. He stared, with intrigue rather than wonder, at the peasant who had experienced the vision, perhaps envying the attention he was garnering.

Raymond raised his hand and waved, acknowledging the people - believing they had assembled to honour him. In contrast, Bartholomew appeared impassive, serene. Other worldly. If he was playing a part, Adhemar mused, he was playing it well.

The crowd kept growing, like a snowball rolling down a hill, even in the short time it took Adhemar to walk across the square outside the church. The bishop started to doubt the wisdom of his choice to unwittingly endorse the "visionary". Adhemar received a message that morning, from Bohemond, arguing that he was exposing himself to ridicule by supporting the peasant. "Bartholomew is as much a visionary as I am a dwarf," the Norman prince posited. "You are setting up the people for a fall, when you excavate the site and find just dirt and shit. And not holy shit either... Be wary of being manipulated by Raymond." There was little that Adhemar disagreed with in Bohemond's letter. But it was too late now to rescind his support. Could the disappointment and anger at not finding the Holy Lance be the straw to break the camel's back? Would the crowd riot? They appeared like they might lack the energy to do so. It was unlikely that morale could plunge any lower, Adhemar drolly thought to himself. But he had concluded that before, only to be proved wrong. The bishop had already composed a few words, akin to a sermon, in preparation to temper the disappointment of the vision proving false.

Crisp sunlight bathed the scene. The whispering crowd parted, with Raymond and Bartholomew at the spearpoint of the distinguished party, near the entrance to the church. Many pilgrims bowed their head in reverence. Adhemar did he best not to screw-up his countenance in revulsion, as he caught wind of the foul-smelling peasants. Raymond posted a half a dozen men-at-arms at the doors to the church, to prevent the mob from entering and interfering with the excavation.

The sun can burn as well as warm. Sweat dripped down his face like beads of wax along a candle. Edward stood upon the battlements. He gazed at the shimmering horizon, past the enemy camp, as though if he stared long and hard enough, he might be able to see England. Home. It's verdant hills, hedgerows and dimpled streams. But all around him the ground was as hard as miser's heart. Yet they had recently been stuck upon the plains of Antioch, as if mired in a bog, he wryly considered.

The knight was temporarily distracted from his thoughts by the sights and sounds of clusters of pilgrims making their way towards the Church of St Peter, like ants heading back to their colony. Perhaps Adhemar was handing out food. Edward felt no compulsion to join them. Churches always made him feel ill at ease. Guilty. He remembered how the figure of Christ upon crucifixes would appear to look at him in an accusatory way. Edward would bow his head in discomfort and shame, rather than reverence.

The wound in his shoulder began to ache again. It would probably hurt like a bastard come the winter, he conjectured.

I'll probably be dead before then though, fortunately or not.

There was a wound which cut deeper, however. The death of his friend, Hugh de Cerisy. Hugh was an honourable knight, if that wasn't too contradictory a term. They had drunk together, whored together. And fought together. The Norman had saved the Englishman's life on more than one occasion, during their campaigning. Edward never knew Hugh to show his back to the enemy. The same could not be said for some of their Frankish allies in the army.

Edward realised that he was standing in the same spot on the walls, when he witnessed Hugh die. It was a couple of days after the sacking of Antioch. A Turkish scouting party, consisting of around thirty horsemen, were observed in the distance. Roger of Barneville, an Italian knight, along with a dozen or so crusaders, including Hugh, were already mounted. Barneville was an admired and accomplished soldier. He rode out, confident of victory, encouraged by greed and glory, despite being outnumbered. Part of his aim was to capture the enemy's much needed horses. Despite their parched throats, cheers vaunted upwards, like church spires, from pilgrims on the battlements, spurring the knights on. Edward silently urged his comrades on too and even pictured himself celebrating with Hugh later in the evening. Defeating the scouting party would feed morale amongst the pilgrims. There was little else to nourish them, the Englishman fancied.

Dust cloud pursued dust cloud, with Barneville and Hugh de Cerisy at the vanguard of the crusaders as they crossed the Orontes. Their fresher horses caused them to close on their quarry. The Muslims retreated. But it was a feigned retreat. A trap. The thirty horsemen turned into three hundred, as the bulk of Kerbogha's scouting force appeared from over the crest of a slope. Having led the charge, Barneville and Hugh were at the rear when the advance became a withdrawal and they raced to reach the safety of the city. The cheers petered out, like a dying storm. A bark turned into a whimper.

Edward gripped his sword and cursed – furious, helpless – as he watched Barneville fall. His back arched as an arrow struck his spine. The Italian knight fell into the shallows of the river. The pilgrims watched in horror, grief and rage as the Turkish horseman who cut him down dismounted, retrieved his axe – and decapitated Barneville.

The Englishman watched in horror, grief and rage as his attention shifted back towards his friend who was being similarly pursued. A hulking Turk, with long black hair, dressed in a bark-brown cloak, on a powerful chestnut mount, ran Hugh down and launched a spear into his back. The weapon punctured his lung. The knight slowly drowned in his own blood, after the Turk stood over the pilgrim and mutilated him. It was the enemy's turn to cheer.

"Bastard," Edward muttered – and he was probably not alone in doing so – as a Turk crossed the Orontes and mounted Roger of Barneville's head on a lance, holding it aloft like a trophy and parading it in front of the watching Christians. Arrows and crossbow quarrels spat in the dust in front of the despicable infidel – but he was tantalisingly, goadingly, out of range. But not for one man. The Welsh archer had known and liked Hugh too. Whilst the men around him shot off missiles and insults, gesticulating wildly, Owen remained calm and coldly went about his business. He stretched out his bow arm and flexed his hand. He took a moment to select an arrow from his cloth bag. He measured the wind just by feeling it brush against his besmirched cheek.

Nock.

Owen let his target settle, as the Turk's slightly skittish horse finally stood still.

Pull.

Edward here observed his friend. The Welshman was the soul of focus. He had rarely seen the archer pull back his weapon so much. For a moment he imagined that the string –

or bow – might break. The knight did not pray or wish the arrow Godspeed. Because he knew he didn't need to.

Loose.

Whispering death. The Turk did not see or hear the arrow coming. Unlike the other missiles launched at him it arced upwards, as opposed to being shot downwards. The arrowhead buried itself into the swarthy enemy's right shoulder. He let out a womanish scream and nearly fell from his once more skittish mare. He clumsily wheeled his mount around and retreated. The Muslim kept his life, but at least he lost his gory trophy.

Hate overcame sorrow, preventing Edward from crying – although later that evening, after half a jug of wine, sorrow overcame hate and he wept in private. He wasn't sure if it was due to being soaked in wine or tears but Edward made a solemn vow, to a God he scarcely believed in, that should he encounter the long-haired Muslim on the battlefield then he would hunt him down and kill him. Show the same mercy to him as he shown to his friend.

The following day Adhemar buried Barneville and Hugh with full honours. Many pilgrims congregated outside the Church of St Peter. The funereal air was palpable, although Edward couldn't quite tell if the crowd were quiet out of a sense of reverence or gloom. Many must have blackly thought how they might soon share the same fate.

Hugh de Cerisy wasn't the first friend Edward had lost over the years to war. And he wouldn't be the last, the knight sadly knew. He thought of Thomas, as the wind began to swirl and howl across the battlements. The lad had made his first kill recently. But that wouldn't mean he would survive another encounter with death.

A team of twelve diggers broke the ground at the spot where, according to their visionary, St Andrew instructed. A few worked enthusiastically, believing that they would discover the famed relic. But most paced themselves, with their heart not being wholly in the task. The sighs they emitted were rarely wistful. The earth was considered sacred – and was collected so it could be returned to fill in the pit they were half buried in.

Raymond of Toulouse jutted out his chin, in determination or expectation, as he stood by the ever-deepening hole being formed in the ground of the basilica. When he noticed any of the excavators flagging, the eager prince would swap them out with a fresh worker.

Adhemar covered his mouth and yawned – again. He continued to compose what he would say to the crowd when, not if, they returned empty-handed. He would ensure that Raymond would not be associated too closely with the failure. He would also not condemn or scapegoat Bartholomew, for fear of the mob turning on the misguided peasant. The bishop winced and asked for God's forgiveness, observing how the consecrated ground was resembling a building site. He instructed the church's chaplain to burn more incense, to combat the increasing smell of sweat and dirt. Adhemar occasionally removed himself from scene - which he couldn't quite decide whether it was ultimately tragic or comic - to glimpse the swelling crowd outside. Growing like a cancer. Many craned their heads to peer inside. He also heard the grating, graceless voice of Peter the Hermit leading some prayers.

Peter Bartholomew remained confident, serene. There was not a flicker of doubt in his bloodshot eyes. He laced his fingers together in front of him and moved his lips in silence, communing with God. His lop-sided beatific smile still steadfastly shaped his countenance, as if nailed on by a blacksmith, Adhemar fancied. Sometimes a shovel or pick struck something hard - or scraped across some gravel. Whilst Raymond's eyes widened and ordered the dig to stop and examine the source of the sounds, the peasant didn't flinch, as if only he could divine whether they had encountered the relic or not.

Dusk simmered. Night would soon descend. Darkness would squeeze out the light. When Adhemar observed the crowd outside the cathedral now they were no longer standing, as if holding a vigil. Instead, they lay on their backs like vagrants or sat on the steps, holding their heads in their hands. Groans often replaced prayers.

Inside the church, hope was similarly withering on the vine. A few princes, such as Godfrey of Bouillon and Robert of Flanders, had visited the site, out of curiosity or otherwise, but swiftly departed – bored or disappointed. Dusk dimmed. Candles and torches were lit.

Raymond increasingly snorted and harrumphed. His chin now buried itself into his chest. The light was fading from his eyes, as well as in the church. What could go wrong, did go wrong, he judged, in relation to the campaign. The count began to consider how he would punish the peasant, should his vision prove false. He would take the clothes back he had gifted Bartholomew and renege on the promise to provide him with additional rations. He would also instruct his lieutenant, Henri of Bayeux, to send the peasant to fight on the most dangerous section of the city walls.

Most of the men, more than waist deep in the less than fragrant pit, looked like they might pass out at any moment. Their tunics and surcoats were as black as Erebus. Their expressions grim.

"We must rest or cease. How long must we dig for? We'll reach Hell before the Holy Lance at this rate," one knight finally asserted, his patience wearing as thin as his belief in the roguish peasant.

"You must dig until you find the relic. Are you doubting our Lord and St Andrew," Peter Bartholomew issued. Adhemar was not the only one to notice how the peasant's voice had grown more nasally – and haughty – since yesternight.

"No, I'm doubting you," the frustrated knight spat back. As exhausted as the soldier was, he would still be willing to muster the energy to knock the conceited commoner on his arse.

"You have toiled hard. You more than deserve a rest," Raymond of Toulouse remarked, holding his hand aloft to signal for others to be quiet. He then called for a couple of attendants to fetch some wine and food, to raise the strength and spirit of his men.

The knights wearily climbed out of the hole, some examining the burgeoning blisters on their hands as they did so. Some offered the peasant a scathing look.

Unperturbed – and undeterred – Bartholomew removed his shoes and the cassock-like garment he was wearing. He proceeded to lower himself into the pit and lifted-up one of the discarded shovels.

"God, grant me the strength to do your bidding. Bishop Adhemar, you are gracious and wise. I would ask you to believe in me – and our Lord and St Andrew – to deliver up the relic," Bartholomew solemnly uttered.

Adhemar shifted uncomfortably. He was not altogether pleased about endorsing and praying for the peasant. He had already been given greater legitimacy than he should have, the clergyman judged. But he did not see how he could refuse the request. When he closed his eyes, Adhemar wished that he had never admitted the "visionary" to his home the night before. He regretted being pulled into his orbit and indulging the charlatan. The bishop recalled a verse from the Book of Proverbs. *"Stay away from foolish people; they have nothing to teach you."*

The setting sun slipped behind the only cloud in the sky and plunged the basilica further into darkness. Adhemar forced himself to say a few forgettable words. Nevertheless, the party duly paused - and the knights bowed their heads.

Shortly after Bartholomew started to dig, his shovel clinked against something. The peasant glanced up at those above him, wide-eyed. He all but licked his lips in expectation. Once he had caught the attention of Raymond, Adhemar and others he bent down and reached into the earth. The triangular piece of iron he pulled out was the size of a large thumb. He brushed the soil from the would-be relic. Time and rust had blunted the edges. It could have been an old spearhead. But only *could* have been, Adhemar thought – having faith in his scepticism. Although there were a few knights who remained silent or narrowed their eyed in suspicion, others gasped with wonder.

Raymond bent a knee (Adhemar couldn't remember the last time his old friend had bowed in deference) and others followed. Even Raymond of Aguilers, a chaplain who was serving as a chronicler for the potential historic moment, stopped writing to process what he was witnessing. The knights, now peering down and circling the hole that Bartholomew was triumphantly standing in, muttered to themselves and one another:

"It's a miracle... God still favours us... Our Father, who art in Heaven, hallowed be thy name... Our prayers have been answered..."

Adhemar stood in wonder too, his mouth agape, that so many people were willing to conclude that they had discovered the Holy Lance and were witnessing a bona fide miracle. Part of him wanted to call out the peasant for being a fraud and swindler. But somehow it wasn't the right time. It would almost be an act of cruelty to challenge such a moment of faith, hope and joy.

"You have handed me victory," Raymond said, his usually stern voice trembling, as Peter Bartholomew carefully passed the holy relic, or lump of iron, to the prince. His aspect was as bright as boy's, after being given his first dagger or sword. "God truly works in mysterious ways."

But not that mysterious, or obvious, Adhemar thought. He quietly questioned whether the count was innocent of Bartholomew's duplicity. Had his own prayer served as a distraction, that the peasant used to plant the piece of iron in the ground?

"Adhemar, are you seeing this?" Raymond continued, cupping the relic in two hands and raising it aloft.

Seeing, yes. Believing, no.

6.

Torn and tortured. Adhemar barely slept during the night. Sweat glazed his brow, his throat grew sore. It was likely he was suffering from the beginnings of a fever. His waking thoughts were as virulent as any nightmare. He told himself he was a coward, for not denouncing the peasant. Bartholomew had deceived people, taken advantage of their despair and faith. How culpable was Raymond in initiating or worsening the profane pantomime? The bishop castigated himself – and asked God's forgiveness – for his cowardice. And now the horse had bolted. Pandora's Box had been opened. Adhemar recalled how, after hearing the news that the Holy Lance had been found, some in the crowd wanted to open the gates immediately – and march out to confront their Godless enemy. The Holy Lance would surely grant them victory.

"Bolts of lightning will shoot out from the divine weapon and smite our foes," one zealous pilgrim claimed.

People became evangelical in spreading, not the word of God, but the word of Raymond and Bartholomew. There was little wine in the city, but the pilgrims acted as if they were drunk.

"The fires of hope and faith are burning bright once more," Raymond boasted at the end of the night, after he reported that many non-combatants were now volunteering to bear arms.

Adhemar couldn't help but consider that, should he challenge the legitimacy of the relic, the truth might extinguish those flames of hope and faith. Talk of victory would turn to talk of defeat once again.

Someone who holds back the truth causes trouble, the bishop mused, remembering the verse from Proverbs. But would he not be causing greater trouble if he revealed the truth? And even if he denounced events, would he be believed? Too many people had already bought in to the deceit. If he advertised the fact that the Holy Lance had been recovered years ago, and resided in Constantinople, would he not be denounced himself? He might be accused of spouting Byzantine propaganda and being an ally of the treacherous Emperor. Or he might be accused of petty jealousy, in response to God choosing the virtuous peasant over the self-important bishop.

An insect bit him. The wind vexingly whistled through a gap in the shutters. His stomach groaned more than an ingrate. The bishop could easily call for his attendant, sleeping in the next room, to prepare him some food. But his clerk, Rainald, needed his rest as well. And Adhemar believed he should suffer. The clergyman felt like he was an accessory to a crime, as culpable as Raymond and Bartholomew. Or more culpable, because he knew better. People can be as fickle as women, Pope Urban had once, perhaps rightly, claimed.

I have no peace, no rest, and my troubles never end, the clergyman thought, now quoting Job.

Eventually Adhemar slept. Not because his soul was at rest, but rather his body was utterly exhausted. The noise from the hubbub on the street outside the house – and the coruscating sunlight slanting through the shutters – woke the burdened bishop. He also woke to a visit from Thomas. Ostensibly the Englishman wanted to return a book he had borrowed, but when he greeted Adhemar he eagerly asked about the Holy Lance.

"Were you present when the relic was discovered? Was the vision real? Was it a miracle?" Thomas remarked, shooting out questions like an archer would arrows. He wanted to believe in the Holy Lance – and would if the venerable bishop told him to do so.

"The world wants to be deceived, so let it. I was present at the excavation site, though I cannot claim to have witnessed a miracle... You are looking at me, slightly aghast, Thomas. But I do not blame you. You are right to do so. I am complicit in a deception. I am not without sin. Perhaps Man should always feel sinful. How else will he be compelled to better himself in the eyes of God," Adhemar replied, philosophically – albeit there was scant optimism in his voice. Thomas thought Adhemar appeared visibly diminished. He was carrying a staff, not just as a symbol of his authority – but to sturdy himself as he walked. At times the bishop stopped, or swayed, like he was traversing the deck of a ship during a storm.

Before Thomas could respond they came out into the square, in front of the Church of St Peter, to be greeted by a sea of people. Heads bobbed up and down. Their joy and devotion were palpable, as if they had already defeated their enemies and been delivered. Knights had polished their armour. Grubby faces had been scrubbed clean. Those who still possessed some semblance of their "best clothes" wore them. Parents hoisted their children on their shoulders. Husbands and wives embraced one another. People greeted the bishop as though it were Christmas Day. There was no better feeling than experiencing a packed church. But Adhemar didn't feel any pride or sense of fulfilment. He considered that starvation, desperation and the shimmering heat were making the pilgrims light-headed. Foolish. Hysterical.

Peter the Hermit had recently spoken to the crowd, in an attempt to give an impromptu sermon. But the congregants called out for Peter Bartholomew to speak. The humble visionary was more than happy to address his flock. Peter the Hermit forced a gracious smile and pursed his lips (if he pursed them any more they may have bruised or bled) – and stepped aside. Bartholomew recounted the story of his succession of visitations, painting a revelatory and dramatic picture with his words.

"...Raymond and our pilgrimage have been chosen by God to bring light to darkness, bring hope where there has been despair, freedom to servitude... The Holy Lance will pierce the thickest armour. We will ride out with God at our side – and ride home victorious. Those who believe in the power of the Holy Lance will be rewarded, in this life and the next. Your sins will be forgiven..."

To describe his expression as self-satisfied, wouldn't quite do it justice, Adhemar thought to himself as he listened to the peasant grip the crowd – like a farmer gripping a chicken's neck - through his miraculous tale and the promise of victory.

Towards the end of his speech Bartholomew began to praise his patron:

"St Andrew commanded, "Follow me and I shall reveal to you the lance of our Father, which you must pass on to Count Raymond, as God set it aside for him at birth." Raymond's faith is as strong as his sword arm. As he believed in my vision, I believe in him. I ask you to believe in him too. Raymond – our courageous commander – will carry the Holy Lance... God has not abandoned us. Raymond will soon lead our army out and we will slay our enemies. God wills it!"

The crowd parted and Raymond ascended the steps of the cathedral, to a chorus of cheers. He carried the spear tip on a silk, purple pillow. The prince interpreted his triumphant reception as being for him, as much as for the relic. Pilgrims stared at the piece of iron with slack-jawed awe. A couple of knights flanked Raymond, to prevent any of the lowly peasants from getting too close to the prince or Holy Lance.

"Praise be to God and Raymond of Toulouse," a voice hollered out. Adhemar briefly glimpsed the figure through the throng and thought the man was part of Raymond's retinue.

The Count of Toulouse instructed his audience to settle. His voice, used to being heard over the clamour of battle, unfurled itself like a flag across the square.

"God is with us. As the vision proved true, that the Holy Lance would be recovered in the basilica, so too will St Andrew's prophecy come to fruition. This lance point you see will serve as a standard, to lead our army against the pernicious infidel. Kerbogha's army will be wiped off the map, as a gust of wind will scatter a mound of leaves..."

Adhemar couldn't hear what the prince said next, as his words got lost amidst the cheers. He forced a smile, yet squirmed in the inside, as a nearby fellow in the crowd remarked,

"This is your victory too, Bishop."

Raymond allowed for a procession of pilgrims to honour the Holy Lance – and himself. A number of overwhelmed people fainted in the sweltering heat as they passed by the relic, staring in wonder. A few claimed to have been touched by

God, after being revived. The Count of Toulouse basked in the moment. Adhemar noticed how Raymond glanced over at Bohemond on more than one occasion, to check his rival was still in attendance. Raymond believed that the Holy Lance had given him the power, popularity and authority to wrestle overall command of the army from the Norman.

Much to his chagrin, Bohemond's expression wasn't as distraught or defeated as Raymond would have liked. Indeed, a flicker of a wry smile played on Bohemond's lips as he took in the scene. The prince would have understandably preferred it if someone, other than his rival, could be credited for discovering the Holy Lance. But Bohemond was still confident of turning a seeming piece of misfortune to his advantage. The relic had sparked a fire. Morale was, miraculously, high again. The pilgrims would now fight, believing that God was on their side. Bohemond didn't believe for one moment in the divinity of the Holy Lance, but he did believe in its power to inspire. The son of the wily Robert Guiscard was no stranger to deception. He had kept his fellow princes in the dark for weeks, as to his plan to infiltrate Antioch. He had also sworn allegiance to the Emperor. But, the day after doing so, Bohemond had toured Constantinople, assessing its defences for when he would attack the city in the future. The Norman nobleman was capable of being honest with himself – albeit he was perhaps less capable of being honest with others – and he had to admire Raymond for his stratagem. Bohemond would have been proud of himself, should he have devised the same plan to motivate the pilgrims and usurp command of the army. But the prince was confident of taking it back. Bohemond was also impressed with the power of the peasant's performance. Should Bartholomew somehow return to Provencal one day, a career on the stage as a lead actor awaited.

"I would like to be there - and observe the look on Alexios' face – when someone tells him that we are in possession of the Holy Lance," Bohemond remarked to Adhemar, speaking in his ear so he could be heard above the general clamour. "He might rush to his treasury to check its contents, for anything missing."

The prince narrowed his eyes, in knowingness and suspicion, as he spoke to the bishop. Adhemar had once commented to Thomas how Bohemond could look at someone and know what they were thinking, just after they did. Or, in some instances, just before. But Bohemond was more amused than appalled that Adhemar had compromised himself and become an unwitting victim of the peasant's scheme. A sinner himself, the prince could forgive sin in others.

"The Emperor's relic might be a fake," the clergyman argued.

"So long as the people believe our one is genuine. They will fight now with hope, as well as hatred. We were always going to have a reckoning with Kerbogha. There will be a battle. But now we have God fighting in our ranks once more. People will choose to fight, instead of being forced to. As much as I would like to hear your account of how you discovered the Holy Lance, I need to take my leave. I must mobilise my company again to stand a watch. Men, as well as the Almighty, must keep us safe. A lump of metal might not be able to repel the Turks, as ruthlessly as we'd like, if they storm the walls. I would be grateful if you could arrange to call a meeting of the Council of Princes. We have much to discuss."

When Raymond began to praise Adhemar – and many in the exultant crowd turned to the spiritual leader of the crusade – the bishop shifted uneasily and wished that the ground might swallow him up. Again, a slither of his weary heart was tempted to speak out and denounce Bartholomew. But it wasn't the time. The time had passed. As many a military commander had told him over the years, during the vicissitudes of war, "We are where we are."

As Raymond addressed the crowd about his renewed purpose to lead the crusade onto Jerusalem and the promised land, the crowd averted their gaze away from the clergyman. Adhemar breathed a sigh of relief, or despair. He welcomed the arrival of Edward. The English knight noticed the strain his friend was under.

"I hear there has been a miracle. Good news travels fast it seems," Edward remarked, his voice laced with irony.

"Gossip is so tasty - how we love to swallow it!" Adhemar replied.

"I've just caught a glimpse of the so-called relic. It's remarkable how much the blood of Christ resembles rust," the soldier said, his tone as dry as dust.

For the first time in some time Adhemar's face broke out into a grin. When he thought of the imminent gathering of the Council of the Princes however the smile fell from his countenance.

7.

Raymond was late for the gathering of the Council of Princes. But he knew that the meeting couldn't start without him. There seemed to be no end to the crowd's adulation. Some of the pilgrims tried to touch the hem of his surcoat as moved through the throng, across the square. After his oration outside the cathedral Raymond instructed Peter Bartholomew that he was not to give any other speeches without his permission. The Count of Toulouse was determined to control the narrative and use of their new, divine, weapon.

The gatherings, between the chief noblemen of the crusade, had been councils of despair of late. Adhemar had led discussions on dwindling food stocks, preventative measures to curtail the spread of disease and ongoing butcher bills. There was also the ongoing issue of desertions. Desperate and frightened pilgrims were still escaping over the walls, lowering themselves down with ropes. Few ultimately made their escape, however. Deserters were being caught, massacred and mutilated by the enemy. The crusaders' severed heads were often catapulted over the walls. The macabre volleys only strengthened the resolve and resentment of the defenders though. As angry and appalled as the Christians were, by the atrocities committed by the Muslims, a few of the westerners were conscious that they were guilty of similar heinous acts. "We are getting a taste of our own medicine," Charles of Anjou had lamentably commented to Edward, when the surgeon treated the knight.

Lavish feasts and fountain-like amounts of wines used to accompany their councils. Delicacies were served by different chefs, in unofficial competition with one another – as if whoever possessed the finest chef amongst the princes possessed the finest army. Adhemar once remarked to Edward that he was only too pleased when the participants gorged themselves. "If their mouths are stuffed with food, then at least they can't speak and squabble." Paintings and banners would hang in chambers, promoting the prestige and family histories of the hosts.

Bohemond was vexed by his rival's tardiness. He sometimes hummed but sometimes growled in thought. As with previous gatherings, Bohemond invited Edward and Thomas to attend. The Englishmen had been briefed beforehand as to what the prince would say. Edward was far from happy about what Bohemond was intending to propose, however.

Godfrey of Bouillon failed in displaying the patience of the saints he venerated. He puffed out his cheeks, tapped his foot and exclaimed that Raymond was being disrespectful and discourteous. As much as part of him wanted to believe in the miracle of the Holy Lance, Godfrey's doubts were as embedded as gallstones. The Christian prince was unhappy at Raymond using God – and manipulating pilgrims through their faith – to make his power grab. As soon as he entered the room, at the rear of Adhemar's residence, Godfrey approached the bishop and questioned him as to the legitimacy of the relic. Adhemar was determined to remain non-committal, which in itself told Godfrey all he needed to know. The prince was sympathetic to the clergyman's predicament. How was Adhemar going to preserve both the crusade's morale and his own reputation? Should he endorse the peasant and his miracle then the churchman might compromise himself in the eyes of some, especially as it was likely that the rogue Bartholomew would eventually compromise himself. However, the majority of pilgrims fervently believed in the relic. It was the bishop's vocation to strengthen rather than diminish faith. For once the crusaders were not drowning in a slough of despond. The Holy Lance offered people hope and the promise of victory. Telling the truth wouldn't.

Robert of Flanders doubted the serendipitous find of the relic, but there would be no doubting his courage when the crusaders gave battle. All that mattered was victory. To live to fight another day. If Raymond was using religion to inspire the people to fight harder, then God bless him, the soldier thought.

Robert of Normandy called for an attendant to re-fill his winecup. He harrumphed on more than one occasion, frustrated by the Count of Toulouse's lateness - as once he arrived, the food would be served.

Tancred de Hauteville was also present. He was young, but as haughty as a figure twice his age, possessing twice his rank. Tancred, his features as strong as his build, had long served under his uncle, Bohemond. But he was tired of being his mere lieutenant. The prince owned ambitions of becoming a king. He was a formidable warrior with a small, formidable army. As much as he owed loyalty towards his uncle, Tancred was willing to be swayed – or bought – by Raymond. Bohemond would duly watch his nephew to assess whether there was any collusion between his kinsman and rival.

Raymond finally arrived. He puffed out his chest, as proud as a peacock, as he strode into the chamber and smiled graciously. Graciousness turned to smugness, as he caught the eye of Bohemond. Thomas observed the two princes. The tension in the room tightened, like a noose around a condemned man's scrawny neck. The temperature even seemed to rise. The Englishman was reminded of a humid night, waiting for its first thunderclap.

The princes sat around a long, creaking table, which looked as ancient as any holy relic. Adhemar sat at its head. He strategically didn't place a chair at the other end, to avoid Raymond and Bohemond arguing over who should sit there. Edward and Thomas, along with representatives from other companies, stood around the table and listened to Raymond make an argument for attacking their enemies immediately, his voice as hard as a gauntlet balled into a fist.

"The Holy Lance will grant us victory. It will make us invincible. God has entrusted command to me. I have heard the call of the Almighty and I will answer it. I will lead our forces out to face the infidel. Our army stands ready. The pilgrims are ready to bear arms. I ask you all to join me – and write your names into the annals of history. I will lead you to victory."

"Or to our deaths," Bohemond countered. He had rolled his eyes and yawned during his rival's oration. "I suspect that I am not alone in being prepared to put my life into the hands of a wine-soaked peasant. Peter Bartholomew could as easily have been sent by the Devil to damn us, as opposed to being sent by God to save us."

It was Raymond's turn to hum cum growl. He could see the likes of Godfrey and Robert of Flanders nod their heads in agreement as his rival spoke.

"This is tantamount to blasphemy from the Count of Taranto. The Holy Lance is as genuine as his faithlessness. May God inflict a plague on such heresy."

"I am not sure I'd notice such a plague, such are the other miseries that have been heaped upon me," Bohemond drily replied, to the odd grin and titter from others in the room. "We must indeed give battle. But in a rational rather than rash manner. It is understandably seductive to believe that the Holy Lance will bestow victory. But forgive me if I'm still wedded to the idea of tactics. I will still be ordering my men to sharpen their swords and tighten the straps on their mail shirts, in case they will need to fight, in the absence of a miracle. I heard the speechifying earlier, outside the cathedral. The boast was that the Holy Lance could pierce the finest armour. I have my doubts that the lump of iron could even pierce a turd."

Again, the Norman's words inspired a chorus of laughter. But Raymond was not beyond scoffing too.

"If not now, when? Every day which passes weakens us – and strengthens our foes. I warrant that Bohemond is suffering from a surfeit of envy, as well as a lack of faith, that God has chosen me, over him, to lead our crusade."

"I have too much pride to allow myself to suffer from envy. If you believe that our victory is inevitable now, it will surely be inevitable in a week or so. We must gather more intelligence on Kerbogha's forces, before engaging them. We need to accurately assess their strengths and weaknesses. I propose that we send an embassy to Kerbogha, ostensibly to officially lay claim to Antioch. The real purpose of the embassy will be to spy on our enemy, however. One of my scribes has been learning the requisite languages to mine information from anything he might overhear. My knight,

Edward, will also accompany the party and apprise the quality and quantity of their troops, where possible. Our enemy may have lost countless men, but they have countless more. We have a slight advantage in that the Muslims will underestimate our martial spirit. Let us not suffer the same error, lest it prove a fatal one."

On mentioning their potential mission – potential suicide mission – Adhemar glanced at the two Englishmen, who he had become fond off. The bishop appeared worried, pained – as if his friends had just been given a death sentence. There was no guarantee that the Muslims would observe the rules of such an embassy. They could be taken hostage or slaughtered, before even having the chance to pronounce, "Peace be with you."

"And will you be deigning to lead the mission?" Raymond asked, picturing a bloodthirsty Muslim beheading the Christian prince as he walked into the enemy camp. The Frank could see the merit of the plan though. Raymond thought that Bohemond's proposal was based on sound judgement, albeit he had spent so long contesting the Norman that he could not wholly embrace any of his rival's arguments. "The son of Robert Guiscard shouldn't be trusted, even when it may be in your interest to do so," Alexios, no stranger to plotting and treachery himself, once advised Raymond. "I have a preference for keeping my head attached to my neck, but perhaps you might volunteer and take ownership of your plan, Bohemond. Or will you be daring to ask one of us to put our lives in Kerbogha's blood-soaked hands? Unless you have a notable figure leading the embassy, Kerbogha may identify it for the ruse it is."

Many of the crusaders around the table lowered their heads, not wishing to signal any enthusiasm for putting themselves forward for the mission.

"I will not be asking any prince to lead the embassy. I have a candidate in mind should we agree on the plan however – and will confirm his participation soon," Bohemond posited.

The likes of Godfrey of Bouillon and Robert of Normandy now appeared intrigued and relieved rather than sheepish.

They had little fervour for putting themselves at the mercy of their bloodthirsty enemy, although they would be happy for someone else to do so if it meant gaining some valuable intelligence.

"As ever, the Count of Taranto keeps us in the dark and asks us to put our faith in him, rather than God. I am ready to marshal our armies now. I freely concede that there are those who will consider giving battle a risk, but it is a risk worth taking," Raymond argued, as he started to calculate in his head how much coin he might need to bribe some of his fellow princes to support his plan.

"Faith is a virtue. But so is patience. I commend Raymond for inspiring a mass of pilgrims to take up arms against our enemies, but we will be leading them like lambs to the slaughter if we do not take the time to train these goodly new recruits. They need to march out clasping weapons, not crosses. We must also ensure we provide fodder for our horses – and build up their strength – before we can ride out with confidence. We must sacrifice some of our food stocks and even donate the straw from our mattresses to this end, else our mounts may collapse beneath us. Many horses are incapable of trotting at present, let alone galloping. We can prepare our troops and mounts during the time it takes us to complete our intelligence gathering exercise. Of course, you could always ask your holy man to petition St Andrew to report on the state of Kerbogha's forces," Bohemond suggested, derisively – the very soul of sarcasm.

Raymond took a deep breath and flared his nostrils, as if he were about to snort fire, Thomas fancied. If the Frank was a simmering pot, he was about to boil over.

"We have sufficient enemies outside the walls. Let us not spark any conflicts inside the city," Adhemar firmly but fairly posited, raising his hand to signal a cessation to any needless bickering. "Raymond, I agree that you should lead our forces when the time comes. You possess the experience and authority to do so. The people will follow you – and you should be given the honour of carrying the Holy Lance. But you must concede that Bohemond is right to be cautious. We all agree that it is a matter of when, not if, we should give battle. We must do everything in our power to allow us the best opportunity to defeat Kerbogha. Bohemond's plan to send an embassy into the enemy's camp to glean intelligence could help tip the scales in our favour."

Raymond remained riled, instead of becoming enraged. He still felt, due the events of the past day, that he was in the ascendancy again. First among equals.

"I believe that the Holy Lance will tip the scales. God is on our side. But I will abide by the decision of the council. Should we vote in favour of the Count of Taranto's embassy, I will support it. I stand prepared to lead the Army of God when called upon," Raymond pronounced, puffing his chest out once more.

"I will bow to the authority of the council too," Bohemond calmly enjoined, because he knew that the council would bow to his will.

8.

Evening.

Edward and Adhemar sat around a fire, which occasionally crackled and spat. A small, rickety table, supporting a jug of wine, sat between the two men.

"Not for the first time during this damned campaign, I didn't know whether to laugh or cry – when Bohemond told me that Peter the Hermit would be leading our embassy," Edward remarked, rolling his tired eyes. "More shit comes out of that man's mouth than out of my horse's arse. Bohemond played him like a lute, apparently. The princes were too wise, or too cowardly, to lead the mission. But the Hermit leapt at the opportunity to play Daniel and enter the lion's den. Bartholomew has stolen some of his thunder – and congregants. He's keen to steal them back. Perhaps the garrulous bastard might talk Kerbogha into submission, bore him to death."

Adhemar permitted himself a shadow of a smile. The soldier's forthrightness was a breath of fresh air for the diplomat.

"One word is seldom enough for Peter, when ten might suffice," the bishop replied, tartly. "Bohemond probably calculated that if he succeeds, he may diminish Bartholomew's – and also Raymond's – prestige. Although the demagogue has been popular among the pilgrims, Peter the Hermit has often irked the princes. If he dies during the mission, they would be pleased to see the back of him. It would also vindicate their decision not to volunteer to lead the embassy."

"Aye, but unfortunately if the Hermit is cut down, then I will be too. I'd rather not queue up outside the gates of Heaven, or Hell, with such a sanctimonious prick," the knight replied, wincing slightly as he sipped from his winecup. The vintage had been diluted beyond recognition.

"How's the wine?" Adhemar asked his guest, noting his expression.

"You've produced a miracle that no one has ever asked for. You've turned wine into water," the Englishman said in good humour. He had to laugh, otherwise he might cry.

"Heaven or Hell will be a less desirable destination should the Hermit start preaching there. That the wine is running out is reason enough for us to try and break this siege. Perhaps if we say that casks of wine await, as well as immortality, then we may prove victorious."

"The promise of some wine and food, for our embassy, in the enemy's camp, was the only reason why I agreed to accompany it," the Englishman said. Neither Adhemar, or Edward, knew if he was being wholly serious or not.

"Unfortunately, Muslims consider alcohol to be a sin, I've been told. Which is reason enough not to want to be an adherent to their religion. I will pray for you, Edward, that the mission is a success."

"I'd rather you expend your prayers on making sure there's some wine or ale there. Should the bastards drink and become loose-lipped then maybe Thomas will be able to obtain some valuable intelligence."

"How is Thomas? He doesn't quite seem himself of late."

"I know. He's been morose, bitter and pessimistic. He's becoming human after all," the knight half-joked. Edward declined to mention how his friend was likely self-flagellating himself, out of guilt for taking a life. The young Christian had been starved of hope and faith, as well sustenance. Edward remembered how Thomas would constantly, fervently mention how he had been present at the historic day at Clermont, when Pope Urban called upon people to take up the cross and join the armed pilgrimage. He also spoke about reaching Jerusalem, "the Kingdom of Heaven" – visiting the Mount of Olives and the Gardens at Gethsemane. He no longer mentioned such things, however.

Emma had given Herleva the evening off. Business was increasingly slow at the brothel. The discovery of the Holy Lance had instilled an unhealthy wave of piety and morality in many of their customers. What money pilgrims had left needed to be spent on food too. Herleva welcomed the respite. She felt like an actress who had spent far too much time on stage. With the young Englishman she could try to be herself, or that self who she wished to be. She wore one of her favourite dresses but, unlike when she was at work, she fastened the garment at the base of her neck. A small wooden cross, which the Christian had gifted her, hung between her breasts. She found herself increasingly fingering the cross and thinking of him, day and night. He was never a slave to his passions or drink, like her abusive father. He possessed a rare and endearing sense of modesty, in more ways than one.

Herleva sat next to Thomas, her hands covering his, in his small room at the house Bohemond had granted to Edward and the scribe. The cot on the floor, covered with a frayed grey blanket, would have been uncomfortable to sleep in even if Thomas didn't have a restless, troubled mind. A rosary, a couple of books borrowed from Adhemar, and a worn stylus sat on a low, iron table with dragon feet-shaped legs. Occasionally the blanket, covering the smashed window, billowed out with the wind. The room smelled of burnt candlewax, damp and the faintest odour of perfume. The cell was cramped - but overflowing with isolation and mould.

The Englishman had never invited his friend to his quarters before. Perhaps he wanted her to see him surrounded by privation and squalor. He wasn't deserving of her, or anyone, he considered – having committed a mortal sin. He deserved to suffer. Yet perhaps he invited Herleva to his room because tonight would be the night for the virginal student to become a man. Tomorrow he could die.

Thomas leaned into Herleva a little. The young woman, one of most popular whores in Emma's establishment, remembered when she had once attempted to clasp his shoulder in a friendly way – and he had recoiled. Before departing for the crusade his mother had taught him to be wary of women, especially "Jezebels". She had always been able to protect her child from the wickedness and wiles of women of ill repute from their parish, who would try to catch her son's eye after church, knowing how wealthy her husband was.

"They are only after one thing... They are vessels of sin. Unclean. Ungodly."

Thomas had been wary, if not frightened, of the "Jezebel" when he first saw her. Was God tempting or testing him? She was drinking and carousing with a nobleman. Due to being within Edward's - and consequently Emma's - orbit he regularly encountered Herleva. His being throbbed with fear, shame and impure thoughts when he was with her. Occasionally he would catch himself staring at her bare legs, shoulders, or the top of her breasts – but then quickly avert his gaze, like a hand retreating from a flame.

Herleva and Thomas had spent more time with one another recently. The scribe was helping to teach the unlettered girl to read. He was always patient and courteous towards her. Unlike other men he never tried to ply her with wine – and then ask her for a discount.

A cloud – or rather another cloud – hung over the despairing youth. Bohemond had told him that Peter the Hermit would be leading their embassy. He was a rabble-rouser and preacher, who lacked scholarship and true piety. There were dogs who were more skilled in diplomacy. Thomas envisioned that their Muslim hosts would gnash their teeth at the zealous, self-titled "Man of God". At best they may be taken hostage and held for ransom, at worst the Hermit could say something ill-judged and they would be cut to ribbons in a heartbeat. The Hermit had led the doomed People's Crusade, having inspired thousands of ordinary Christians to join the pilgrimage – and whipped them up into a frenzy to deliver death and destruction against the Jews ("Christ's killers," as he judged them). Perhaps only Pope Urban himself had recruited more souls to the campaign. People followed the hair-shirted Hermit – but he led many to their deaths, as if his words were a siren song, before they even reached Constantinople. "I will remain faithful to you, if you remain faithful to me," the Hermit often pronounced, his hand splayed across his breast in heartfelt conviction. Yet Thomas grew nauseated when he heard the demagogue spew out his sermons, as he was party to the knowledge that the Hermit had once attempted to desert his flock – and had to be hunted down and dragged back to Antioch by Tancred de Hauteville.

And so Thomas anxiously tapped his foot as he sat next to Herleva. Or he tapped his foot from suppressed lust, excited to feel the girl's body next to his. Smell her moreish perfume. The virginal student told himself he was curious about sex, on an intellectual level. His mother had drummed into him that sex was a religious duty, in order to procreate, rather than a source of pleasure. "Lust is a deadly sin," she dictated, priest-like. He always thought that he would wait to be married. His first time with a woman would be in a cottage on his father's estate, on his wedding night. But Thomas also recalled Edward's words on the subject: "If you're not enjoying it then you're not doing it right."

Herleva squeezed Thomas' slightly trembling, slightly perspiring hands.

"Can you not refuse Bohemond's request?"

"I would have more chance of turning night into day, I fear. Bohemond is not a man to be refused. No, I will do my duty," the translator replied, with a distinct lack of enthusiasm. "I just hope that the Hermit is capable of doing his duty too."

Thomas swiftly forgot about the preacher however as he raised his head and Herleva's features loomed large. Her almond-shaped, sultry eyes now radiated with kindness, making them even more beautiful. He needed to tell her he wanted to spend the night with her. Be with her. He didn't want to die without first being intimate with a woman. But his shyness was crippling. The words remained stuck in his throat, like a warped blade stuck in a scabbard. Herleva too was fettered. For once she couldn't be so brazen. The woman didn't want to die without first telling a man that she loved him. And he could die tomorrow. But Herleva feared that if she made an advance he would retreat – and never come back.

A dog barked in the background. Perhaps more of a desperate yelp than a bark. Thomas darkly considered how the creature would not survive the night, if caught. Pilgrims were eating rodents. Dogs would be a delicacy. He wryly smiled at the grim thought. Herleva believed he was smiling at her – and reciprocated. Thomas realised how much he liked her. But did he love her, like he had loved Yeva? He believed that he had loved Yeva, that he was destined to save her. She had been the niece of Varhan, who had helped Bohemond gain access to the city. The Armenian had made the Englishman promise to protect Yeva, after entering Antioch. Thomas dreamed about the girl and composed poems about her. He believed she was calling to him through his dreams, as God had called to him at Clermont to take the cross. Unfortunately, the dream, or God, proved false. When he reached her house during the night of the sacking, he found her dead. A piece of him died too. He kissed the cold brow of her corpse. A bunch of crusaders had raped and murdered her, despoiling her virtue and beauty. Her beaten countenance, her eyes swollen with terror and pain, still haunted him. Thomas felt like he was a widower, who had never been married. If he pledged himself to Herleva he would somehow be being unfaithful to Yeva – and he couldn't then be with her in the next life. Atone for his sin of not saving her.

"Edward won't let anything bad happen to you," Herleva said reassuringly, with more conviction in her voice than in her heart. But her smile was now forced and faltering. "I will pray to God to watch over you too," the woman added, fingering the cross around her neck.

Thomas reciprocated the forced and faltering smile, but the translator remained lost for words. His blade remained stuck in its scabbard. The knot in his stomach wasn't just due to starvation.

9.

The corn coloured sun blazed in the shimmering sky. The air itched, stung. A patina of dirt and dusk permeated everything. The Muslim camp, once a hive of activity and flashing blades, was limed in a state of inertia. Soldiers lazed around, brushing the flies away from their faces and staying out of the stifling heat.

Kerbogha knitted his brow and stroked his chin in apparent disquiet, as he hunched over the chessboard. More of his pieces resided off the board rather than on it. His opponent, Balduk of Samosata, licked his lips – in expectation of tasting victory. Inside, however, Kerbogha was grinning triumphantly. The commander always planned several moves ahead. Kerbogha realised that, within just eight moves, he could trap Balduk's king and prevail. Several other emirs had observed the game unfold and stood around the board. Where before they had fawned over their general and praised his prowess, most now doubtless wanted him to lose, Kerbogha considered. They thought he was arrogant. But the Atabeg of Mosul had cause to be arrogant. Kerbogha would happily disappoint his allies and snatch victory from the jaws of defeat. Chess was everything. Winning nourished him. He had played since a child and over the years he had employed tutors from India, China and France to help improve his game. Chess instilled focus, patience and ruthlessness. Only a fellow chess obsessive could understand how he played out matches in his mind before sleep – and even dreamed about games. When he wasn't playing, he would habitually carry a chess piece and rub his thumb over the intricate carving. He liked the sound of the pieces clicking against a polished wooden board, especially when it was a fast-paced game.

Kerbogha finally made his move, after his ruby-ringed hand hovered over several different pieces in seeming indecision. The finely crafted set was carved from ivory - although the infamous commander didn't dispel the rumour that the pieces were formed from the bones of his enemies.

The two men had been playing together now for several months. As Kerbogha had once deliberately lost a match to the Sultan of Baghdad, he wondered if Balduk was deliberately losing to him, in order to ingratiate himself with his superior. It was doubtful. Apparently Balduk was plunged into a foul mood after each defeat, whipping his slaves or mistress in frustration. The nobleman, who fancied himself as a military strategist as well as an accomplished chess player, always played aggressively. Too aggressively. He was as predictable as the cycles of the moon, or a Christian's perfidiousness.

Balduk took in his opponent. He was enjoying his discomfort, watching him sweat. His usually calm, cold, hawkish expression was absent. His smooth features were creased in anxiety. His glossy black hair, which was regularly oiled and perfumed, appeared a little bedraggled. Yet a neatly trimmed beard still lined a slender – but strong – jaw. His eyes may have flitted around the board in concern – but normally his aspect was dark, determined and intelligent, full of scrutiny and suspicion. Balduk judged that he wouldn't be the only one to savour the victory, or rather Kerbogha's defeat. His fellow emirs didn't have as much faith in their commander as Kerbogha had in himself. They should have taken Antioch by now. Balduk wasn't alone in thinking that their general was hesitant in launching an all-out assault on the city – and putting it to fire and the sword – because he aimed to possess Antioch for himself. The Christians were holding out longer than expected. The bloodletting was continuing. Good Muslims were being sacrificed, like pawns. Kerbogha stated, every day, that they would triumph "eventually". But "eventually" needed to come sooner. Whispered criticism abounded – and would soon become more audible. Could Kerbogha now fail to capture Antioch, as he had failed to capture Edessa? Could Bohemond and the pilgrims remain resolute – and prove victorious – like Baldwin? For weeks the great Muslim force tarried outside of Edessa (partly because their rapacious commander had heard rumours of a great riches behind the city's walls). Should they have marched directly to Antioch they would have caught their enemy out in the open and slaughtered them immediately. But, due to their commander's greed and strategic misjudgement, the westerners had been given a stay of execution. Kerbogha's plan was to now encircle the enemy and starve them out, after being unable to break through the westerner's lines through the citadel. Despite being recently resupplied, however, the Muslim army were beginning to feel the bite of hunger - and having to ration food. The murmurs of discontent were growing more voluble.

Balduk moved quickly, as soon as his opponent removed his hand from his piece. He advanced one of his remaining pawns, intending it to reach the opposite end of the board. He would then create a queen – and the match would then be all but over. Would Kerbogha be willing to surrender and concede the game, or fruitlessly play on and suffer death by a thousand cuts? Balduk consumed another sweet pastry, content to witness either of those fates.

A rare breeze wafted through the open-sided tent, bringing with it the moreish aroma of the spiced lamb which Kerbogha's personal chef was cooking, on the nearby grill he had set up. Perhaps the general didn't quite appreciate how much others were starving because he was still eating so well, the Emir of Homs had suggested to his fellow noblemen.

As well as a fragrant breeze one of Kerbogha's lieutenants, Radwan, entered the tent. Each large stride was accompanied by a chinking sound, from the expensive mail shirt the fearsome warrior wore. The hulking Muslim turned his bullneck a little, left and right, to take in the others in the room. He inwardly snorted in derision at the decadent emirs and parasites present, who were proving more of a hindrance than help to his master. Radwan had once fought under the Sultan of Baghdad. But he shifted his allegiance – and not just for the pursuit of gold. It is better to worship the rising rather than the setting sun. His master was the future. As well as serving as a military commander under Kerbogha, for more than five years, Radwan also ran a network of spies, which dealt with potential enemies both in and outside the camp. The dedicated Muslim also happily took on the duty of being the army's chief interrogator. Captured deserters, who had escaped from Antioch, were brought before Radwan. He took great pleasure in extracting both information – and pain – from the dishonourable crusaders. The latter helped generate the former. Even when he had wrung every atom of intelligence from his prisoners, the loyal lieutenant would inflict torture for torture's sake. The Christians were a stain on the land, which needed to be eradicated.

Radwan's face, marked with smallpox scars, was as hard as flint, his eyes as black and merciless as a shark's. His dark hair hung down, mane-like, over his round, muscular shoulders. A large, talon-like hand gripped the bejewelled hilt of a scimitar which hung from his waist. The weapon, which had cut down scores of enemies over the years, had been a gift from his paymaster. As was the amulet which dangled around his neck. The rumour was that the ornate piece of jewellery contained a list of enemies, which its wearer had vowed to vanquish. Radwan had led the scouting party, which had first reconnoitred the city. The lieutenant had sprung the trap of enticing Barneville and his knights out from Antioch with a small force, to then overwhelm the crusaders. Radwan had also instructed one of his troops to taunt their foes, by mounting the head of one of their victims on a lance and brandish it in front of the heathens.

"The westerners have sent out an embassy, under a flag of truce," Radwan said, or rather spat out. Contempt ran through his voice, when he mentioned the enemy, like grain running through wood. "What would you like me to do?"

Should Kerbogha ask him to, the lieutenant would be willing to soak the flag of truce in their foes' blood. Although the warrior usually believed that a man should abide by the rules of war, the dishonourable Christians didn't deserve such treatment.

Kerbogha knitted his brow further, either in thought or vexation - that his game had been disturbed, just as he was about to dispatch his opponent.

"Perhaps the curs have finally resigned themselves to their fate and have come to negotiate their surrender."

It was about time, the commander considered. His probing attacks, bloodying their enemy every day, had finally taken their toll, Kerbogha surmised. The intelligence, from the deserters they captured, suggested that even the nobles in the city were starving. They had slaughtered many of their animals. They were drinking the blood of their horses. The pilgrims were boiling leather for stew and picking the remnants of food out of excrement. The only thing they had left to swallow was their pride. Morale was non-existent. Or it should have been. Yet still they proved as resilient as cockroaches, or rodents. For some reason the pilgrims even found their voice again and jeered at their opponents yesterday. They seemed emboldened, for some unknown reason.

Could his dream, of seeing his banner fly over the royal palace, finally become a reality? Kerbogha had interpreted his vision as a prophecy. Taking Antioch would renew his prestige and authority, after his failure at Edessa. Any surrender would have to be unconditional. It was checkmate. He would put Bohemond and Raymond of Toulouse in chains – and parade them before his army like slaves. He would force them to denounce their God and praise Allah. He would permit Radwan to indulge his desire to drop scorpions down the throats of the leading Christian noblemen. His lieutenant was also keen to force a serpent into an infidel's mouth, to see if he could choke a man to death in such a manner. To win favour with the emirs the commander would allow them to take the best of the western women, to fulfil their perverted appetites. He would allow his soldiers to satisfy their bloodlust and greed - and let them slaughter, rape and thieve for a day and night. Ideally Kerbogha wanted to preserve the city, however. If he could somehow trick his enemy into coming out onto the plains of Antioch, he would. The ambitious general planned to use the walled city as a base of operations – as a new Baghdad, Alexandria or Jerusalem – to establish his own kingdom and take the fight to the Byzantines and the West.

And eventually his Muslim brothers in the East. Kerbogha was now the Sultan's subordinate. After taking Antioch – and Edessa and Aleppo – he would be the Sultan's rival. But eventually, the general envisioned, the Sultan would bow before the soldier. Eventually couldn't come soon enough.

Kerbogha's success was predicated on the demise of the crusaders. Should the embassy presage a surrender, he would wipe them off the board.

10.

Most of the party appeared decidedly glum, like they had just been diagnosed with leprosy, when the embassy made its way out of Antioch. The figure at the head of the dozen or so strong group was glowing – beaming – however. He had been willing to swap his donkey for a destrier. The preacher told himself that it was his destiny to save the pilgrimage. God – as well as Bohemond – had selected him for the mission. Raymond of Toulouse had gifted the commoner some expensively dyed robes, to grant the Hermit a greater air of rank and authority. As much as some in the embassy considered the preacher to be a joke, their enemies needed to take him seriously.

"His weeds may be fine, but he's still a sack of shit," Edward remarked to Thomas.

Rumour had it that Peter the Hermit preached with such vehemence, for Christians to take up the sword and the cross, because of a previous failed attempt to go on pilgrimage. Some years ago, on the road to Jerusalem, he had been abused and assaulted by a band of Seljuk Turks. They had beaten him, robbed him and forced him to eat his own faeces, to a chorus of laughter. When the Hermit now preached that man should love his fellow man, he didn't mean that such love should be extended to the Turk. "They are a breed apart," he pronounced. His philosophy of universal love and mercy also failed to encompass Jewish people too. Adhemar reported to Edward how the Hermit had been personally responsible for torturing and killing Jews, as his "People's Crusade" travelled through across the continent. "He has blood on his hands, for the massacres in the Rhineland," the bishop asserted. "Keep an eye on him during your embassy, Edward. Peter Bartholomew may be deemed more trustworthy. The Hermit abandoned his own followers, leaving them to the mercy - or lack thereof – of the Turks, after they crossed the Bosphorus. As you know, he also tried to desert during the siege of Antioch."

"My worry is not that he'll abandon us, but that he'll remain," the Englishman replied, pursing his lips before and after.

"Let them wait and let them sweat. Keep them penned in, like animals waiting to be slaughtered," Kerbogha remarked to his lieutenant. He would be focussed, patient and ruthless. The commander had instructed Radwan to be polite to the embassy and say that the general would attend upon the party soon. But equally his lieutenant should be inhospitable. Their guests should be neither watered nor fed. They should be guarded and left out, exposed to the sizzling heat.

Kerbogha worked his way through his plate of spiced lamb, licking his lips and fingers. He initially felt disappointed – and slighted – that the embassy was being led by the lowly figure of Peter the Hermit. He had hoped that he would encounter Bohemond of Taranto. Was he as tall as he was famed to be? He wanted to look his opponent in the eye, as if he were sitting across a chessboard from him. Kerbogha was also keen to size up Raymond of Toulouse. One of the deserters revealed the magnate was much diminished, through age and exhaustion. He was defeated. He just didn't know it yet, his enemy judged. Yet Kerbogha realised that Bohemond and Raymond were wise not to lead the embassy, as he would have been tempted to execute them – to inspire applause from his followers and dread in his enemies. Bohemond, in particular, was a threat. Sooner or later he would need to cut off the head of the snake.

Edward felt like he was a slab of meat, being braised in the afternoon sun. If looks could kill, the surrounding Muslims, glowering at the exposed westerners, would have murdered him a hundred times over. The Englishman still managed to raise a corner of his mouth in half a wry smile, recalling how Bohemond warned him that Kerbogha might keep the embassy waiting, to test their strength and patience.

"Why do I think this? Because I would do the same. I'm a bastard. I'd be astounded if Kerbogha wasn't a bastard too."

BESIEGED

The image of Bohemond in Edward's inward eye was replaced once more by the figure of the Muslim Goliath, who had brusquely ordered the embassy to wait inside the small, exposed square area – marked out by rope and knee-high posts. Sneering, armed guards kept watch and barked out warnings, brandishing blades, if their charges moved too close to the cordon. The brawny, craggy-faced Muslim who had imprisoned - or quarantined – the party was the same figure who had cut down Hugh de Cerisy. On first encountering Radwan, Edward rashly thought about drawing his sword and skewering the Muslim, without a word said. He pictured himself mounting a nearby horse and racing back to the city. The knight had made a vow – a sacred vow – to avenge Hugh. But Edward needed to honour his friend, as well as avenge him. He wouldn't be doing so, however, if the rest of the party, including Thomas, were condemned by his actions. It made his teeth itch and soul burn to see the man who had killed his friend alive – and holding power over him.

To ease his anger the knight collected his thoughts, concerning his mission. The enemy camp was sprawled across the plains, like the crusader army had been when they had besieged Antioch. And as with the Christian force, the Muslim soldiers often dragged their feet - their faces appeared haggard and some looked like they might collapse under the weight of their armour. Edward couldn't help but note that, whilst the pilgrims often congregated around cooking pots and drank, the enemy chanted and prayed. *If they drank more they might laugh more too*, the Englishman considered. The camp was populated by plenty of soldiers in their prime, but Kerbogha had conscripted in callow youths and greybeards to enlarge their numbers. Such troops wouldn't stand if attacked. Or, if they stood, they'd fall if charged, Edward calculated. Tellingly, as well as glaring at the crusaders with scorn, there were some who eyed Edward with fear.

Edward was not alone in thinking that their quarantine would have been more bearable if they didn't have to suffer the company of their designated leader. Peter the Hermit's expression fluctuated between being pinched and pious.

Initially he paced up and down inside the cordon, asking and demanding to see someone in authority. He prattled on, grating Christian and Muslim alike.

"I am an emissary, sent by the Council of Princes and God... We are here to negotiate with Kerbogha of Mosul... I insist that you treat us with the respect we deserve. Do you not know who I am? What is your name?! Tell me who your superior is."

The Hermit utilised Herluin, the official interpreter for the embassy, to speak to the Muslims. Even before entering the camp, Herluin was habitually as jittery as a broken-winged bird, located next to a foxhole. The young scholar had entered the seminary, but he left after disgracing himself with a senior priest. Herluin volunteered to join Robert of Normandy's company, after hearing a sermon by Pope Urban, serving as a clerk and translator. He was a studious and important part of the nobleman's retinue. Robert of Normandy first used his linguistic skills to negotiate the purchase of supplies across the regions, before the foraging parties began to steal provisions from farms and villages. He possessed an angular, anguished face. Bushy eyebrows sat above bulbous eyes, a narrow nose and thin lips. Herluin may have lacked confidence, but not competence – and he duly translated the Hermit's words.

Sweat poured off the nervous yet indignant preacher. He bit his black nails till they started to bleed. He had envisioned being fed and feted during the important diplomatic mission. The brutish guards remained stone-faced in response to the animated, self-important infidel. Or they smirked at him. The Hermit eventually became breathless and planted his arse on the baked, dusty ground. He soon mumbled and complained to himself however – before beginning to pray. He then proceeded to ask his fellow pilgrims if they would like him to pray for them – and if they had any food or water to spare. Some generously shared what little food and water they had. If he was drinking and chewing, at least there would be a blessed respite from him speaking.

"Would you like me to do anything for you, my child?" Peter the Hermit paternalistically remarked, leaning over a

Lotharingian, who appeared several years older than the preacher.

"Yes, piss off and stay silent," Conrad snapped at the mithering clergyman, echoing the thoughts of others.

Peter the Hermit backed away, as if a dog had just growled at him, and stewed in his humiliation and resentment. As God-fearing as the clergyman was, he was even more frightened of the knight at that moment.

Thomas welcomed the quiet. The demagogue had been babbling as loudly and incessantly as a river. The translator could now turn his attention to the two noblemen who approached the westerners, who had come to cast their eyes over the pilgrims as if they were at a menagerie, viewing exotic animals. Thomas pretended to be oblivious however to the visitors, as if they were speaking gibberish.

"For their sakes, I hope they are going to announce their surrender. The less blood they spill of ours, the less we may spill of theirs. The devils must be desperate and starving. When we finally enter the city, we might see the streets already littered with corpses. They will be skin and bone. The maggots will have little to feast upon," Matar of Harran remarked, laying a chubby hand on his pot belly as he spoke. His leather-brown skin glistened with perspiration. His face was round, fleshy and child-like. Emerald eyes peeped out through feminine lashes. The Muslim thought the pilgrims feral rather than ferocious.

"I hope they surrender for our sakes too, my friend. It is not only my men's stomachs which I hear grumbling in the camp. Deaths and desertions will rise, like vines climbing up walls. Kerbogha should have already taken the city. The Prophet would have vanquished the enemy by now, swatting them like insects. Kerbogha says that he has time on his side. He also has over thirty thousand troops on his side to defeat the pilgrims. Our general seems more concerned with playing chess however – and planning his next move in setting up his kingdom. But I have no desire to merely be a pawn in his game. Once we have dealt with the westerners it is my intention to return home, with my army, immediately. I never thought I would say such a thing, but I miss my wife," Toghtekin expressed, as he stroked his long, black, silken beard – which tapered down to his naval. In contrast to his companion his countenance was lean and hard.

"And I miss my mistress," Matar replied, ruefully. The nobleman sighed, as he thought about how much he missed the courtesan's cooking, as much as her prowess as a lover.

11.

Kerbogha would have been content to see the westerners wait and suffer some more, but he finally summoned the embassy to his tent. He didn't want to lose the light, in relation to the sport he had planned. He was also understandably keen to hear what the pilgrims were going to say. He did not dare hope, but today could prospectively be the final day of the siege.

Several emirs sat either side of the Atabeg of Mosul on cushioned chairs. Kerbogha's chair was positioned on a raised platform. Careworn slaves stood in front of a long banqueting table, ready to serve, like soldiers ready to advance, once their master gave the order.

The weary and wary pilgrims were slack-jawed and near salivated at the foodstuffs and drinks on the table when they entered. Plates of olives, spiced meats, flatbreads, cheeses and sliced fruit were on view, as well as jugs of water and goat's milk. Hunger pangs afflicted the starving, sunburnt crusaders – as if someone were stabbing them repeatedly, like it was the Ides of March.

A flustered Herluin mustered what dignity and propriety he could to explain how he would act as the translator for his envoy, Peter the Hermit. Kebogha, the soul of civility, first apologised for keeping the westerners waiting, but he explained that he had important matters to attend to. He was now free to host his guests however – and they were welcome to help themselves to the victuals laid out for them.

"We have plenty to spare," the general boasted, lying through his freshly cleaned teeth.

Herluin translated the Muslim's words as best he could, sweating due to the heat and anxiety of mistranslating a word or phrase and causing a diplomatic incident – and getting them all killed.

Without waiting for their envoy's permission, the pilgrims immediately took advantage of their host's hospitality. They loudly gulped down cups of water and gorged on any food within reach of their dust-caked hands. Toghtekin whispered to Matar that their guests resembled pigs next to a trough. Matar barely heard his friend however, as watching the pilgrims eat made him hungry.

After the food was consumed the pilgrims stood before Kerbogha and the emirs once more. The imposing figure of Radwan stood to the side but glowered at each visitor in turn – catching their eye and intimidating them, as a lion will stare down his prey. Only Edward did not avert his gaze. He remained unflinching, unyielding. Defiant. Even goading. Bohemond had warned his knight about drawing attention to himself during his time in the enemy's camp.

"Be anonymous. Observe, rather than be seen."

Whether due to his pride or anger though the Englishman could not, or would not, subjugate himself and be intimidated by the hostile Muslim. *Better to die on one's feet than live on one's knees.* But pride can come before a fall. Kerbogha covertly noticed the silent exchange between the two seasoned warriors.

Herluin duly introduced his envoy, but Peter the Hermit felt compelled to introduce himself too. Fortunately, or not, his verbosity replaced the shards of tension in tent.

"I am Peter of Amiens, son of Renauld L'Ermite of Auvergne. You may have heard me more famously referred to as Peter the Hermit. I am the chief envoy of the crusade to liberate Jerusalem. I am a priest, a man of God. Bishop Adhemar may officially be the spiritual leader of our campaign, but I am the People's Priest. Come, keep up Herluin. But don't translate that I said to keep up. On the day that I received the news of Pope Urban's sermon in Clermont, God called me to take up the cross. I preached the gospel of the pilgrimage, inspiring commoners and nobles alike. Followers flocked to me – followers from afar a field as England, Flanders and Lorraine. They were inspired by my words and the Holy Ghost. I led the People's Crusade. I think that Kerbogha might like to hear how I gave orders for Jews to be punished and the Torah to be burned, as we journeyed eastward. If he asks about the fate of the People's Crusade, then change the subject. But subtly. But tell him this. My masses and ministry have provided great comfort and wisdom to my fellow pilgrims. My congregants desire to kiss my ring and the hem of my garments…"

Thomas wondered whether Kerbogha's pronounced yawn was feigned, or real, as he listened to Peter the Hermit ramble on, like an actor looking to build up his part. Worried that there was no end in sight to his preamble the general raised his palm and interjected.

"You are here to present a proposal, I imagine, Peter of Amiens. I suggest you do so, before nightfall."

Herluin translated the words, although there was hint enough in the Muslim's expression which communicated his intent.

"Yes, of course," the pilgrim replied, his voice cracking, not just due to his parched throat. He bowed his head in an apology to his displeased host and took a breath, recalling the words which Bohemond had instructed him to deliver.

Herluin translated, the blood draining from his quivering face. Bohemond ordered the scribe to pass on the correct message, even if the envoy didn't. The diffident interpreter knew what was coming – and feared what might come afterwards.

"Our leaders and commanders are shocked to see that you have been so bold and vainglorious as to enter this land, which belongs to the Christians. Perhaps you have come hither with the full intention of being christened? Or have you come to make yourselves a nuisance to us in any way you can? In any case our leaders, as one man, require you to remove yourselves from the lands, which belong to God and the Christians – for the venerable Saint Peter converted it long ago to the faith of Christ by his ministry. The Council of Princes hereby grant you permission to take away all your goods, horses and mules, camels and asses, and to take with you all your sheep and oxen and other possessions whithersoever you may choose," the preacher exclaimed, his voice growing clearer and stronger as he progressed, as if he were delivering a sermon from a pulpit.

Kerbogha's eyes widened, in shock and animus, as Herluin translated the pompous envoy's phrases. He desired defeatism, not defiance. His chest heaved up and down, like bellows, and his hands increasingly gripped the sides of his chair. Despite his burnished skin his knuckles grew as white as coral. Most of the emirs creased their countenances in disgust and displeasure, like they had just swallowed rotten dates. They could scarce believe what they were hearing. The Christians were mad. Thomas observed others however, who smiled a little behind raised hands. Were they smirking at the Christian's folly, or at the insult to their general? A leader should be loved or feared, but never laughed at, Thomas considered.

"We neither want nor like your god and your Christianity. We spit upon you and your flock. We have come here to remedy the insult of you laying claim to our lands. Do you want to know our answer to your offer? Then go back and tell your people that, if they do not renounce their god and bend their knee, they will all be slain or put in chains, to serve us and our children in everlasting captivity. You should be begging for favourable terms, rather than trying to dictate them. Tell whoever sent you, to spew forth your risible words, that the conquerors will soon be conquered. You are already dead. The Prophet wills it. Your God has abandoned you, as has Alexios. Your brethren are also daily deserting your cause. We scoop them up, like fishermen their catch, each day. We will follow the teachings of our sacred Quran, in regards to our enemies. "Slay them wherever you find them - and drive them out of the places where they drove you out." Tell Bohemond that I look forward to twisting my sword around his innards and disembowelling him. Letters will be sent back to your insidious Pope Urban, written in the blood of Bishop Adhemar. Your people will convert - or die terrible deaths. You have brought the vengeance of Allah upon yourselves," Kerbogha exclaimed, or roared. Veins throbbed in his forehead. Spittle issued forth, like sparks from a sharpening stone – unable to tame his rage and offence. The general was now standing upon the raised platform, towering over the

Hermit like a dragon, about to smite him. For the first time the pilgrim regretted his decision to lead the embassy. The glory of God, and the adulation of the crusade, were not worth the dread he felt right now. His intention was to make the exploits of Peter Bartholomew a fading memory. The vainglorious priest had no desire to become a fading memory himself. He was fearful of the infidel drawing his sword and cutting him down – and the clergyman was also scared of emptying his bowels in front of everyone. Peter the Hermit opened his mouth to reply, but he merely emitted a croaking sound, like a death rattle. Edward wondered whether the demagogue might just be playing dumb. The knight had been present when Bohemond had briefed his envoy.

"You must mention nothing of the Holy Lance and change in morale. If your tongue lets slip, then I'll remove it on your return. God knows there are plenty of people who would like me to do so, even if you don't transgress during the embassy. Remember, as much as you may be there to spy on them, I will ensure that there are those who spy on you," Bohemond instructed, as adamantine as the shield of Achilles.

Peter the Hermit remained mute. Kerbogha was not so lost for words, however.

"You will be the first to bow down before me. Kneel!" the commander bellowed, as if he were issuing orders during the cacophony of battle.

Although the general directed his order at Peter the Hermit the majority of others in the crusader party fell to their knees, fearing that the Muslim's ire might turn towards them afterwards. Edward remained one of the few pilgrims still standing. Kerbogha flashed the knight a baleful look. His lips receded over his gums, like a dog who was about to bite, but Edward appeared amused rather than admonished. Kerbogha, snorting as opposed to breathing, was initially going to punish such insolence. But he couldn't help but admire the soldier's pluck. The general decided to regain his composure.

Thomas didn't quite know whether Kerbogha's wry smile was feigned or not, as the Muslim took in and addressed the truculent knight. Herluin, who constantly wiped his perspiring palms on his tunic to try them, continued to translate.

"And who are you?"

"Edward. A knight. From England," the crusader replied, neither politely nor rudely.

Kerbogha waited for Herluin to translate, turning his back on the Hermit as he did so, before responding:

"England? I have heard of your far-off land. I have been told that it's awash with rain. I have met a few Englishmen over the years. But what are your women like?"

"More appealing, after a couple of cups of ale. They're preferable to the women north of our border, however. Not even a jug of wine could make those creatures seem more attractive, or thinner. Aye, it does rain in my country. But I must confess that I've started to appreciate my climate more, after experiencing yours," Edward drolly countered.

"It is not only wet weather which afflicts your country. You were conquered by William, a Norman, were you not? The Normans slaughtered many of your kinsmen, I imagine – and stole your lands. But yet you fight for your enemy," Kerbogha asserted, trying to goad the westerner. "What do you say to that?"

A few of the emirs sniggered and smiled in satisfaction, at hearing their general's words.

"Inshallah," Edward replied, shrugging his shoulders. Not rising to the bait.

A few of the emirs now let out a gasp of shock - or spat out curses at the blasphemous infidel. The goaders became the goaded. Radwan was willing to slit the heathen's throat, with just the merest nod of the head from his commander.

Somewhat surprisingly though Kerbogha let out a burst of laughter.

Herluin, whose reedy body and breathless voice seemed to be trembling in equal measure now, continued to translate.

"I can't quite decide whether I like or detest you, Englishman. Perhaps it's possible to do both. You must be drunk, stupid or brave to blaspheme in such a way in the presence of so many Muslims."

"Perhaps you will get to find out what I am if we meet on the battlefield, should our negotiations not go according to plan," Edward remarked. A flintiness infused his humour. He briefly considered how he might be being irritating – and irritable – due to not having any wine or ale for too long a period.

A hardness, or gleaming malice, permeated Kerbogha's tone and aspect as he unflinching addressed the insouciant, or impudent, westerner. The veneer of civility, masking a deep-seated barbarity, was growing thinner by the moment as Kerbogha warned his enemy, in a far from coded way, as to what might be his fate.

"I remember the last Englishman I met on the battlefield. I captured rather than killed him. He was a former Varangian. His armour may have been polished, but not his manners. He possessed an insolent tongue, right up to when I cut it out. I flayed his back, like an errant slave, so the bones could be seen glistening beneath his skin. Radwan here cut off his ears and forced him to eat them, although he was so hungry by then that he would have consumed them anyway, I believe. The Varangian stood as tall as you – but by the end he was reduced to acting like a dog, crawling around on all fours. Whimpering. Begging."

Kerbogha permitted himself a smile, or sneer, as if he had just discovered he was ten moves from checkmate – whilst the unsettled interpreter passed on the Muslim's grim words. But Edward was never one to know when he was beaten.

"You need to tell our host something, Herluin. Something he seems to have forgotten. Every dog has its day."

12.

After threatening torture and death towards the English knight Kerbogha dramatically changed his tone and proposed some "sport". Edward couldn't quite tell if the general tricked the Hermit into agreeing to the contest. He asked the pilgrim if he believed in honour. "Do you not have faith in your God that you will triumph?" Kerbogha suggested that the two sides put forward a champion to compete in combat. "Both men can wear their armour of course, to prevent serious injury. Though the rules of combat will apply. I possess a sand timer, which will limit the duration of the contest. I will provide further hospitality during the sport." Edward considered that, rather than being tricked, the Hermit was just bowing to the inevitable. He was at his host's mercy – and Kerbogha the Dreadful was far from merciful. There was no turning back from the road they were on.

When Kerbogha announced that he was putting forward Radwan as his champion, Edward was keen to participate in the contest. Before he could do so however the envoy volunteered Conrad to represent the crusaders. The Hermit had briefly thought about choosing the veteran English knight, who he knew to be a fierce competitor, but he did not want to return to Antioch and greet Bohemond with the news that he had been responsible for losing one of his prized soldiers. He also relished ordering the Lotharingian to take part, in revenge for Conrad humiliating him earlier in the day. Thomas sadly mused how priests were not immune from pettiness and vindictiveness. His faith had waned, in men and religion, since setting off on the historic campaign.

Godfrey's lieutenant duly accepted the challenge.

Kerbogha clapped his hands and rubbed them together, in response to the envoy accepting his proposal, and declared that there was a suitable space which his soldiers used for practising their swordsmanship halfway across the camp. The party set off, with Kerbogha whispering conspiratorially in his lieutenant's ear.

The sun continued to pummel the earth in a dry heat. Odours (some pleasing, some less so) prickled his nostrils. Edward walked on - along the ruts that had been created in the hard ground, connecting different parts of the camp. *When you're going through hell, keep going.* Despite suffering a certain amount of trepidation as to what might unfold Edward welcomed the opportunity to observe more of the enemy's camp. The first thing that struck the knight was that they had the numbers to overwhelm the pilgrims. That was almost all that mattered. *Almost.* The westerner ignored various scathing looks and took in an archery range on his left. A few bowmen were drilling themselves properly and hitting their targets. But the majority of troops seemed lethargic. Edward knew soldiers – and knew when they possessed fire – and food – in their bellies. They were not defeated, but many were disgruntled, he suspected. They were as frayed as the flights on their arrows.

Conrad estimated that Kerbogha would not have proposed the contest, without believing that his champion would triumph. But the knight would back himself. The Lotharingian had put many a man, Muslim and Christian, to the sword throughout his life. He had been the only man in the company to defeat Godfrey in a practise combat bout. He had bested bigger and better than the lumbering brute ahead of him, Conrad reasoned. As much as he could endeavour to kill his opponent, the soldier judged that he should hold back. If he ended the Muslim, then he worried that the entire embassy might earn their host's wrath. Although Conrad was confident of surviving the contest the devout Christian still offered up a prayer to God to aid him in his cause.

Fear aided him in his assignment, Thomas believed, as he walked through the camp, close to – but not too close to – several emirs. He wondered what a group of emirs should be called. A wealth? No one would consider the young, timid pilgrim a threat – if they even noticed him. The scribe - or spy, he might now title himself – even tried to appear a little gormless as he covertly caught what exchanges he could between the enemy.

"Kerbogha isn't as noble as he thinks he is, nor is he as flawless a military commander as he would like to have people believe. War isn't a game of chess," the Emir of Homs sniped to the Emir of Menbit. "He is also turning into a war profiteer. He is lending provisions and funds to the Emir of Aleppo at such an exorbitant rate as to make a usurious Jew blush."

"I am beginning to think that we are beginning to spill our blood not for the divinity of the Prophet or security of our people, but for the glory of Kerbogha," the Emir of Menbit replied, shaking his head in supercilious disapproval.

Thomas listened to what snippets of information he could take in from soldiers congregating around cooking pots. One group gesticulated wildly, sawing the air like bad actors or over-zealous chaplains, as they argued the merits of Kerbogha's strategy.

"The infidels must be on their knees. We should deliver the killing blow. We should attack through the citadel once more. Allah will be the divine wind at our backs, driving us on to break through their defences," a downy-faced youth exclaimed.

"You wish to wash away the stain of Muslim blood through needlessly spilling more? It may not be as glorious as you would like, letting disease and starvation kill off the heinous westerners, but it is wise," a hawk-nosed greybeard asserted, sitting on a prayer mat. He sighed, rather than gesticulated. The veteran had seen plenty of deluded young men keen to fight before. And he had seen plenty of deluded young men die, in the name of Allah.

The spectacle generated an ever-swelling audience, even without the numbers Kerbogha's attendants drew in from spreading the word throughout the camp. Some of the crowd began to move up and down and rhythmically chant Radwan's name. The hum of prayers could also be heard. A few spewed out insults in the direction of the pilgrims, herding themselves together in an ever-tightening group. Or the holy warriors declaimed verses from their sacred *Quran*:

"O Prophet! strive hard against the unbelievers and the hypocrites and be unyielding to them... The punishment of those who wage war against Allah and His messenger and strive to make mischief in the land is only this, that they should be murdered."

Edward noted a few fading bloodstains in the sand. Thankfully the makeshift arena was large enough for Conrad to be able to manoeuvre around in, should the Saracen get the better of the knight. Or if the pilgrim started to get the better of the Muslim, there was space to retreat into. Should the Lotharingian kill his opponent then the baying crowd might tear the crusaders limb from limb, like a pack of hounds.

"Don't worry, Edward. I am aware that if I win this bout then we could all lose," Conrad said, measuredly. "I will endeavour to provide some entertainment for our hosts – and at the same time avoid embarrassing our side. I am as keen to get back to the city as you are. I used to curse the walls of Antioch when we stood out on these plains. Now that we are behind them though I am happy for our priests – and even that preening fool over there – to bless them."

"Take care, Conrad. I have every faith in your ability. But Kerbogha wouldn't have proposed this bout if he wasn't confident of the outcome. Keep away from the crowd, skirting the space, as they may try to trip or strike you. And I trust that big bastard, about as much as I can throw him," Edward replied, eyeing Radwan with unbridled hostility.

Kerbogha adopted an air of ebullience as he addressed the crowd, circled around him.

"We have been visited by an embassy from the infidels. Let us welcome them. The next time we see our foes will be when they bow before us and surrender... They have agreed to some sport, before they return to hide behind their walls once more... The scimitar will give battle, against the western sword... Praise be to Allah. May the Prophet grant Radwan victory, as a show of strength for what will come."

Victory would raise morale and provide a welcome distraction for his bored and frustrated soldiers, Kerbogha judged. The small triumph might even quieten the carping of various emirs. They still made reference to Edessa, with seeming relish.

The sounds of whispering, like air rushing around in a seashell, filled the air as the throng speculated upon why the westerners had visited the camp. Were they opening negotiations to surrender? Who was present? Some pointed at Edward, mistaking the tall Englishman for Bohemond.

Occasionally a breeze kicked up dust and caused people to cough. The sound of the Orontes, slapping against the bank, could be heard in the background, prompting a desire for many to quench their thirst. Throats were parched, as if they had all recently swallowed a cup of sand.

The crowd parted, allowing the combatants through to the open space, and then moved back into their formation. Many stood on tiptoe and craned their necks to gain a better view. Conrad felt like he was being cooked in his armour, although he remained a sea of calm – of stoicism and Teutonic imperiousness - amidst the storm of antagonism around him. Fists punched the air. Abuse was hurled, like children throwing food at a party. But the knight stuck to his task. He took on plenty of water. Adjusted the straps on his armour. Practised strokes with his sword. Envisioned the ways he would move around his lumbering opponent – and strike. Droplets of brackish sweat wended their way down his nose and rested on his upper lip, where he licked them off.

Radwan tied his long hair back. He swung his arms around, windmill-like, to stretch them – and helped whip-up the crowd in a further frenzy. A further cheer went up when he brandished his large scimitar. The curve in the blade increased the length of its destructive edge. But the point beats the edge, Edward told himself. The Englishman also consoled himself with the fact that Conrad didn't need to win. If David could slay Goliath, the crusader could survive the imminent encounter. Edward couldn't help but be drawn back again, like water being sucked down a drain, into recalling the image of

Hugh de Cerisy being killed by the brute standing a dozen paces away. Should the Hermit have called upon him to take part in the contest he might not have been able to prevent himself from aiming to kill the man who had murdered his friend.

The juddering clang of the two blades crashing together snapped Edward out of his reverie. Out the corner of his eye he witnessed Herluin flinch at the sound, which set the translator's teeth on edge.

Kerbogha had raised an arm and then lowered it, to commence the bout. He also turned his sand timer upside down. Thomas couldn't be sure, but he thought the sand timer currently in Kerbogha's hand was larger than the one he displayed back in the tent, when he proposed the competition. The torrent of cheers buffeting Thomas meant that he could no longer discern any conversations taking place. He didn't envy Conrad, having to survive even a moment combating the fearsome Muslim.

Edward's features dropped. Radwan's strength and power were impressive, but unsurprising. The shock came from the swiftness of the large warrior. Despite his size, despite the weight of his armour, he moved with equal speed to his opponent.

The knight deflected several blows, but he retreated as he did so. He was clearly experiencing difficulties. Peter the Hermit felt a brief pang of guilt for having volunteered Conrad for the contest. He began to think about what Godfrey of Bouillon might say, or what he might do to him, should they return to Antioch with his lieutenant seriously injured. Or slain.

Sweat drenched his face, like he was suffering from a fever. Conrad briefly tried to glance at the sand timer, still being held aloft by Kerbogha, in the hope of it nearly running its course. There was an age left it seemed though. The Muslim was an accomplished swordsman, far more skilled than he predicted. The Lotharingian thought he would have to fight to save his pride. But he would now need to fight for his life.

The knight retreated. But his opponent wouldn't allow him any respite. Radwan advanced. Although genuinely breathless, the crusader made his breathing appeared more laboured. He lowered the tip of his sword, as if too fatigued to hold it fully upright anymore. He wanted his opponent to believe he was beaten. Radwan smirked, revealing a set of crooked, yellow teeth.

As when a cornered animal might suddenly spring forward, in a last bid to break free or attack, Conrad suddenly advanced, thrusting his broadsword at the same time. He was quick. But not quick enough. Radwan moved to the side, letting the blade pass harmlessly by him. With skill and speed, he moved forward himself and butted his opponent. The blow smashed the crusader's cheek bone and the bridge of his nose. Conrad was stunned. The world was a blur. And it soon turned to darkness. Radwan lined the blade of his scimitar along an exposed part of the pilgrim's neck, above his armour, and sliced open his carotid artery. Blood gushed out, like water spurting from a broken pipe. Cheers drowned out any gasps emitted by the Christian embassy. A chilling, gurgling sound filled the air as Conrad brought his hand up to his wound, but the blood easily poured through the gaps of his gauntleted fingers. Edward raced towards his fellow knight, but he collapsed and passed out before he reached him. The Englishman felt helpless, like he was watching out over an ocean and seeing a ship slowly sink in a squall. Not even Charles of Anjou would be able to help him now, Edward thought. Only God could save the crusader. But God had been conspicuous by his absence for some time.

Edward closed the dead knight's eyes, mostly because the Englishman felt uncomfortable with the perceived accusatory look he received. The Lotharingian mouth was contorted in agony, like he had suffered a seizure. Edward told himself that the pilgrim was in a better place, for Antioch was close to being hell on earth.

The knight glanced at his countryman. Thomas looked like he was going to be sick at any moment. Edward never felt as far away from home as he did now. He wondered if Thomas felt the same. It was unlikely that either of them would make it back to England. Edward even darkly mused that no one now would return. The pilgrims would either be slaughtered or enslaved.

Edward next turned his attention to Radwan. The warrior was basking in his triumph, soaking up the adulation of the crowd like the rays of the sun. Grief was, just about, sovereign over Edward's sense of rage. When Radwan noticed the knight, he grunted derisively and then grinned, goadingly. Edward was tempted to challenge the Muslim to single combat in another contest. But his task now was to prioritise the safety of the embassy and venture back to the city. It also dawned upon the westerner that he might not be a match for his opponent. The edge could beat the point once more. If he was challenged though he would answer the call. He had, like Conrad, his pride. But pride can come before a fall.

Repetitive, thumping cheers assaulted Thomas' ears, accompanied by a chorus of howls. He thought what they were saying was a variation on *Allahu Akbar*. But he didn't know - and he didn't much care. In some ways he envied Conrad. At least it was now all over. He would no longer starve or suffer a tortuous disease. Or feel fear or distress. He wouldn't endure the blistering heat or numbing cold. Thomas worried that the exuberance of the crowd could spill over into violence against the Christians. Although sober, the Muslims were behaving as if they were drunk. They might soon savage the party like a group of Bacchants, he fancied.

Kerbogha barked out an order to Herluin, to attend to him. The scribe obeyed, as if the general were his master. Kerbogha ignored the embassy's chief envoy and approached the English knight. He was a paragon of feigned sincerity when he expressed his grief at the sad demise of Conrad.

"I am sure he was honourable. But Allah willed his death. Your dog did not have his day," Kerbogha remarked, with a flicker of a smile. "This sport should serve as a prediction for what is to come, if our two armies give battle. We both know that we have the numbers. You should make peace with your God, Englishman. For we will not make peace with you, unless you surrender unconditionally. If you deliver that message to your Bohemond and Raymond of Toulouse."

Whether due to his raw fear, or the dryness of his throat, Herluin's voice cracked as he conveyed Kerbogha the Dreadful's message.

"I will. But I can give you our answer now. We will not submit, even if your Allah wills it. You have the numbers. But it's not about the size of the dog in a fight. It's about the size of the fight in the dog."

Light began to drain from the sky, as the colour began to drain from Conrad's countenance. Thankfully the Hermit remained dumbstruck - whether frightened or grief-stricken - and didn't interfere as Edward mustered the doleful embassy. The knight asked Thomas and others to help him carry their fallen comrade. He didn't want to leave the body with their enemies, to deface and desecrate. More than most, the Lotharingian deserved a Christian burial.

The pilgrims were mocked – and sometimes even spat upon – as they made their way back through the camp. Fatigued. Despondent. Despairing. Edward turned back one last time to stare at Radwan. Neither man needed Herluin to interpret what they thought of one another.

13.

A gibbous moon hung in the night sky, like a silver brooch askew on a widow's funeral weeds. Edward, exhausted both spiritually and physically, had wanted nothing more than to see Emma when he returned to Antioch and the gates closed behind him, reverberating like the noise of the door to a gaol slamming shut. The sight of her, the sound of her voice, the taste of her kiss, would serve as a balm. He wanted his body to slot next to hers, feel the warmth of her perfumed skin, and fall asleep. Edward didn't even want to dream. He just wanted to be dead to the world. But Bohemond had instructed his knight to call on him, with Thomas in tow, as soon as the embassy returned.

Peter the Hermit was ready to address his congregation. But there was no welcome party to greet and cheer the embassy. Perhaps the rest of the pilgrims knew that there would be nothing to cheer.

Thomas trudged behind Edward as they made their way through the fetid, gloomy streets of Antioch. He felt like he was wading through the noxious marshes, which bordered part of the plains. He moved as if someone had hold of his ankles, trying to drag him down to hell. Edward slowed his pace, so as not to leave his friend behind. He glanced back and tried not to look too piteously on his companion. His expression was haunted. Any number of things could be haunting him, Edward mused. His shuffling gait was more akin to an old man than youth. A few spots of blood still freckled his right cheek, from where Conrad's blood had sprayed out from his wound.

Bohemond had spent most of the day calling upon his fellow noblemen. He offered to supply funds and provisions – and asked them about how many of their horses were fit to ride out or could be fit to ride out soon. He proceeded to slyly, or overtly, intimate that he didn't think that Raymond was the best candidate to lead their armies into battle.

"...The Holy Lance has addled his wits. I fear that such is his over confidence, he will throw caution to the wind and endanger us all. He keeps zealously positing that he should carry the relic at the vanguard of our forces. I say let him. I would much prefer to carry a sturdy shield and sharp blade. But we cannot let Raymond assume overall command."

It became apparent to Bohemond that he was preaching to the converted. The likes of Robert of Flanders and Robert of Normandy didn't need much convincing (Bohemond left his nephew Tancred off his list, fearing that his loyalties now lay with his rival). It was good sense, rather than poison, he poured into their ears, as he re-filled their winecups with one of the last vintages he possessed. As much as the princes knew that Bohemond could be vain-glorious and self-serving – and wished to undermine his rival - there was no doubting his abilities as a military commander. The Norman had beaten the enemy before – and he represented their best chance to beat the enemy again. Raymond's glory days were behind him.

Bohemond went on to assert that many people had suggested to him that Adhemar should be the one to bear the Holy Lance. If asked to name just a few of these "many people" he would have struggled however to come up with more than two (with one of them being himself).

Candles flickered. The noise of rats scratching and scurrying in the loft above filled the air as Edward and Thomas entered Bohemond's chambers. Thomas noticed that the damp patch, from a leaking tank, had increased in size since his last visit. Water dripped with irritating monotony in a bucket on the floor. Bohemond noticed Edward take the sight in.

"Once I fix something in this damned house, something else falls apart. I'm swimming against the stream. But I'm used to it. I probably shouldn't repair anything now, just in case I need to hand the property over to some gloating Turk, or Kerbogha himself. I'd rather leave them with a steaming turd than the smell of fresh paint... You look tired, my friends. But I'd prefer to see you tired than dead."

Bohemond called out to an attendant and offered what hospitality he could spare. Edward appreciated the wine – and not just because he was thirsty. The prince sat with a corrugated brow next to a table with a map upon it, displaying a plan of the city with an array of crosses marking out the crusader armies and the various enemy camps. Sufficed to say there were more crosses located outside the city walls than inside it.

The two men made their reports. Bohemond expressed some sadness over hearing about the loss of Conrad, although he calculated that the intelligence gleaned was worth the death of the knight – albeit the Norman would diplomatically refrain from conveying that thought to Godfrey. Bohemond listened with intent and occasionally interjected, to ask a pointed question or make a comment.

"They are understandably better provisioned than us, but they are beginning to suffer. Let them suffer some more. We still need time to prepare our horses and provide some basic training for the pilgrims who have volunteered for military service... It's heartening that the enemy may be more disunited than us, if that's at all possible. It seems that Kerbogha's manifest failure at Edessa still festers like gangrene. The stench of defeat is difficult to wash away. And did we not defeat him at the foot of the citadel? As strong as their faith is in their Prophet, they may be losing their patience in relation to their general... There may be chinks in their armour. There are plenty of grey beards – and no-beards – in their army. Many of their troops will be green. Their swords have been stuck in their scabbards for so long that they may not know how to draw them. I have heard that Kerbogha is fond of putting his inexperienced troops in the front ranks, to blood or sacrifice them like pawns. We must turn this mistake into a fatal flaw. If we can rout the front ranks, they will withdraw and trample upon the veterans at the rear. Our cavalry must wash over them like a tide. Like a tide of blood. It's why we will need every horse available. We must pray that our knights take the pawns off the board... And did our envoy behave himself? Kerbogha will indeed underestimate us if he thinks that Peter the Hermit represents the best of us," Bohemond remarked, as he rhythmically ran a sharpening stone along the edge of an ornate but deadly dagger. "Look after your blade and your blade will look after you, far more than any friend," his father had advised the young nobleman many years ago, during their first campaign together.

"He behaved as you might have expected, but eventually he put his tongue under lock and key. Our host prompted him to do so. If he hadn't, I fear we still might be listening to the garrulous rogue introduce himself," Edward replied, doing his best – but failing - to suppress a yawn. As long a day as Bohemond had endured, the knight's had been even longer.

"For once the holy fool has proved useful – although seeing how far the commoner has come, he may not be as foolish as we think. Acting as an envoy has enhanced his reputation. He has been able to polish his pride, whilst Peter Bartholomew's has dulled. The numbers of their relevant flocks may increase or decrease accordingly. Thankfully I don't get involved in such petty feuds," Bohemond said, with a knowing smile, as the three men thought of the prince's rivalry with Raymond of Toulouse. "I hope that Kerbogha felt duly offended, that I would send such an ignoble creature to talk to him as an equal. Our message and obduracy riled him it appears. In short, what did you think of our opposing commander?"

"He's devious, ambitious and arrogant," Edward replied.

"A man after my own heart then. Although I suspect he is after my head even more – and to liberate it from my body. If you permit me to be as garrulous as the Hermit for a moment, my friends. I once killed a man in battle by choking him. I had seen the Greek bastard kill one of my men and I was determined to pay him in kind. I had lost my sword in the melee. I knocked him to the ground. His throat was bare, neither protected by a helm or armour. My large hands easily encircled his scrawny gullet. I got to look him in the eye as I choked the life out of him. His bloodshot aspect bulged – and threatened to pop out of his sockets like scallops. His arms and legs thrashed for a while like a drowning man might flail one last time, before the sea finally swallows him up. His tongue lolled out, at an angle, like he was possessed by an evil spirit. His eyes pleaded with me, substituting for a torrent of words.

My hands continued to crush his throat, however. I imagine I must have appeared as if possessed by an evil spirit too. Mercy could go hang. His strength ebbed out of him, like a retreating tide which wouldn't come in again. He died a horrible death, thirsting for one last sip of air to prolong his wretched life. I recount this incident to you because the enemy is now pinning us down and choking the life out of us. But I will not be slowly strangled, starved to death. I will lead our armies out and give battle, living or dying by my sword. More than God, or some rusty lump of iron, we should have faith in ourselves. You say that their numbers are over three times our own. But our men are worth more than three times that of our enemy. I have sacrificed too much to capture Antioch, to hand it over to Kerbogha without a fight. No retreat, no surrender," Bohemond remarked determinedly, with thunder on his brow.

The young scribe was too tired to be afeared or inspired by his commander's words.

He'll either deliver or damn us.

14.

"You cannot negotiate with a lion, with your head in its jaws," Adhemar conceded with a sigh, after Edward provided his friend with a report of the previous day's events. The bishop would support Bohemond's plan to take the fight to the enemy – before the enemy, or rather starvation, defeated them without a fight. "We are dealing with Kerbogha the Dreadful, not Kerbogha the Clement."

The clergyman rubbed his temple, although there was not a massage or poultice in Christendom which could soothe his headache. Adhemar considered that, at best, most of the pilgrims would perish in any battle. But it was still preferable to all the pilgrims, including the women and children – the innocent souls – suffering.

Victory lied somewhere between being unlikely and impossible, Adhemar mused. As despondent as it sometimes made him, the bishop would regularly climb up to the battlements and survey the Muslim camp, unchristianly wishing ill on his opponents. He owned a special spyglass and would attempt to reconnoitre things. Gain knowledge of the enemy. But he who increaseth knowledge increaseth sorrow. The enemy had the numbers to annihilate them. As well as looking out across the plains of Antioch the bishop would note the occasional corpse of a deserter at the foot of the walls, as they died falling whilst attempting to escape. A few would only break a limb, but then have their throats slit by the enemy under the cover of darkness. Adhemar saw such a corpse in the distance that morning, but as well as installing a sense of the tragic in the clergyman it also inspired a kernel of an idea which could help Bohemond defeat their foes.

His steps were leaden - and his head was bowed in grief, not prayer, as Adhemar took his walk along the walls that morning. His thoughts were as black as a starless night as he flirted with the idea that it was the Devil, not God, who had called out to him on that fateful day at Clermont. He imagined what his friend Urban would be doing. It would be easy for the Pope to preach of the justness of their cause, half a world away from the siege. How the light of God and civilisation were migrating eastwards – and chivalry was defeating barbarism. He imagined his mentor conferring with his congress of cardinals, debating esoteric theological points or discussing policies to increase the coffers of the church. They would be eating from a table that even Charlemagne would have envied.

"You have seen their camp at first hand Edward – and I trust your judgement. Do you believe that we can prevail?" Adhemar asked, before coughing.

"After a few cups of wine, I might be persuaded to say yes. If I said no though, that doesn't mean that we do not have a chance. And some losing battles are still worth fighting," Edward replied. The English thought how he was not fighting for the glory of God or to reach Jerusalem, or to secure the road to the Holy City for pilgrims and wealthy merchants. He was not even fighting for money. He would be fighting for Emma and a life together after this bloody madness. And he would be fighting to avenge Hugh and Conrad. If he spotted Radwan on the battlefield, he would challenge him. If he carried out the latter though Edward realised that he may not be able to fulfil the former. If he fought the Muslim, he could end up second best. And second best wouldn't be good enough.

"They may be the only battles worth fighting."

Again, after he spoke, Adhemar let out a hoarse, spluttering cough. His skin was clammy. Edward's mother would have said that the bishop was starting to look like "death warmed up". The Englishman's expression couldn't help but signal concern for his friend.

"It's nothing. I'm fine," Adhemar explained, lying.

As Edward soon after took his leave he heard Rainald advise his master that he needed to rest.

"No rest for the wicked," the bishop wryly countered. Before coughing again.

Honey coloured sunlight poured through the window of the Church of St Jude. Thomas preferred the small, intimate place of worship to the Church of St Peter, especially since Peter Bartholomew seemed now in permanent residence, preaching and recounting the scene of him uncovering the Holy Lance. Thomas mused that should he be back in England right now such sunny weather would be considered a blessing. His village would be dressed in their Sunday best clothes. People would be clinking cups of frothy ales together. But in Antioch such balmy weather was described as normal – or infernal.

A familiar musty odour permeated the church, which had been restored to something resembling its former glory by Bishop Adhemar. A faint trace of incense still hung in the air, but whereas the smell used to be aromatic it now seemed acrid to Thomas.

His attention was drawn towards an old man in the corner, who appeared to be suffering from some form of palsy. His hand trembled as he tried to light a candle. Once the candle was lit however his shaking hand extinguished it. A hooded stranger, who had been praying before a crucifix at the front of the church, approached and helped the elder. He shared a few words with the greybeard and handed him a quarter of a loaf, which he retrieved from a cloth bag hanging over his shoulder. Although Thomas couldn't be wholly sure he thought he recognised the Good Samaritan as he walked by him to leave. It was Godfrey of Bouillon. The prince was capable of kindness, as well as killing.

Shortly afterwards the old man shuffled down the aisle as well. The wrinkled, rheumy-eyed pilgrim forced a fond smile as he caught the youth's eye. Thomas forced a smile in return. Even if they were all close to their Judgement Day, courtesy should still be king.

Thomas used to enjoy attending church, whether with others at mass or by himself. Before Antioch he had prayed daily and devoutly. But the pilgrim currently shifted uncomfortably on his knees, unable to pray. He struggled to recall his favourite psalms and Bible verses. It was as if they had fallen out of his mind, like coins falling out of a purse. Behind a mask of politeness, intelligence, there was despair. Necrosis. He wanted to pray, to learn how to pray again. But any such prayer would have been half-hearted at best. He wanted to find some peace. Grace. Some faith. Some love. But he felt as if all those things were in the past, if they even existed in the first place. God had abandoned him and Yeva. Should he not abandon God in return? God had abandoned their crusade too. The pilgrims needed to be rewarded in this life, not just the next. In one last desperate effort Thomas clenched his eyes shut and pressed his hands together, almost until they hurt, and tried to pray. He could still recite the Lord's Prayer. He had been reciting it from as early as he could remember. He could even recite the words in five different languages.

Our Father who art in Heaven.

But seems absent from this world. Do you remain in Heaven, not deigning to visit this charnel house? Are you content to let Peter Bartholomew perform miracles for you?

Thomas heard a few footsteps sound upon the besmirched flagstones, but he carried on with his prayer.

Hallowed be thy name.

Your name has been consecrated, made holy. But by who? Man? Is Man capable of making anything holy? Man is only capable of desecration - and cheapening everything he touches. Nothing is sacred anymore.

The scribe recalled how Peter Bartholomew would only commence his "tour" of the basilica once his flock had deposited a sufficient offering of victuals and coin.

Thy kingdom come; thy will be done.
On earth as it is in Heaven.

But what is thy will? What is thy kingdom? Why have you created more questions than answers? If we should bow down to your will then we do not have free will. But if we only have free will – and your will does not exist – then all is meaningless.

It was at best comical, at worst sacrilegious, to allow the likes of Peter the Hermit to interpret the kingdom of God and His will. If God's will is being carried out on earth then is God vengeful, as opposed to merciful?

Give us our daily bread.
You are now incapable of even this. Just one miracle would provide succour.

The smell of the burning candles and incense reminded Thomas of the corpses burned in the city, from people dying daily of starvation.

Forgive us our trespasses.
But you are not forgiving us. You are punishing us, for trespassing in foreign lands.
As we forgive those who trespass against us.
But why should you forgive us, when we are incapable of virtue and clemency? We besieged this city and slaughtered its inhabitants. Would it not be just now for our sins to revisit us?

Thomas' face briefly creased itself up in grief, as if he were a child about to cry, when he remembered Yeva. He was honest with himself and God. He couldn't bring himself to forgive whoever killed the innocent woman.

Lead us not into temptation.

Thomas thought of Herleva. Her bare flesh. He also considered how Christians had been tempted, in God's name, to take the cross.

But deliver us from evil.

Evil seemed as real, hard, substantial, as the stone he was kneeling on. But goodness was as ethereal, wispy, as smoke. Or non-existent. All was vanity under the sun. Evil was omnipresent, like God. Death was the only deliverance.

For thine is the king, the power and the glory.
For ever and ever.

Thomas felt an urge to scratch his balls. Perhaps he was still thinking of Herleva still. But a thought soon skewered him, nauseated him. But still he held it in his mind, like he was gripping a hot coal. It had been drilled into him that Man was God's creation – and that He loved his creation. But what if God was Man's creation? Was that why Man still loved God?

His eyes hurt, from clenching them shut.

Thomas couldn't bring himself to say "Amen".

Night. Darkness visible. Clouds smeared the sky like scabs, snuffing out the light of the stars. Edward welcomed the gloom, in order to complete his task without being observed by the enemy.

The corpse he carried over his shoulder was so fresh that it hadn't even acquired the smell of death. Most people were rotten to the core when living, but perhaps this poor soul wasn't, Edward considered. Even in death the pilgrim, who had perished from starvation and illness, might be able to do some good and save lives.

The knight could feel the man's pronounced ribcage – and noted his twig-like fingers and that the pilgrim had made more than once extra notch on his belt. Edward put the body down, dressed finer in death than he had been in life, and snapped his neck, before dropping the corpse over the battlements.

"Godspeed."

The thud as the body landed at the foot of the walls sent a shudder through the knight's bones, but he quickly shook it off. The enemy would spy the body in the morning, believing that a deserter had suffered a fatal accident, and then retrieve it under the cover of darkness. The Muslim troops would doubtless search the bag for any valuables or food. They would also discover a letter however, which would hopefully find its way into Kerbogha's hands. Planting the letter was Adhemar's idea. It contained information on the discovery of the Holy Lance, which the supposed deserter was convinced was genuine. Adhemar hoped that word could spread among the Muslim camp and take advantage of their superstitious nature. The missive, which was written as a letter intended for the dead man's brother back home, also shared the news that rations were running low, but that the crusaders possessed sufficient food for the next week. After that the princes would try to negotiate a surrender. "They will seek terms, no matter how unfavourable or dishonourable... If I stay, dear brother, I will die." The letter ended with a plea that, should someone find the crusader's message, they would try to deliver it to the address enclosed.

The purpose of the ruse was to convince Kerbogha to cease any probing attacks on the city over the coming week or so. It was not worth the enemy sacrificing any more pawns, if the pilgrims were about to surrender. Even pawns have some value. If Kerbogha took the bait, then their attack would also come as a greater surprise and the enemy would be ill prepared.

Bohemond had endorsed Adhemar's plan.

"My father would have been proud of such a ruse," the Norman remarked. Bohemond often wondered whether his father would have been proud of him, in light of how the campaign had progressed. He would have doubtless accused his son of overreach. Jerusalem was a dream. The real prize was Constantinople, he would have hammered home. Robert Guiscard, cautious as well as sly, would have retreated before being cornered. His father had been a sixth son, a mercenary who had fought his way, blood trailing in his wake like slime secreting from a snail, to become Duke of Apulia. Bohemond asked himself, why shouldn't his disprized heir rise to become King of Antioch, or the Emperor of the Byzantine Empire?

Edward couldn't tell if it was down to the wine he had imbibed, but he gently closed his eyes and offered up a brief prayer that Adhemar's letter would reach Kerbogha. He would likely never know if the ruse worked. He just had to have faith. The knight made a pact with God in the malodorous darkness – a sacred promise. Should God spare him - and he survived the imminent battle - then the soldier would march on to Jerusalem. Perhaps the wine hadn't been as diluted as much as he thought. Or perhaps Edward concluded that it was unlikely he would be alive to honour his side of the deal. Therefore he could promise the world.

15.

Sweat poured down his face as if it were being wrung out like a wet rag. His arms ached and felt stiff, like unoiled cogs rubbing against each other. Thomas tried to picture the images of knights – and their various stances and the positions of their swords – that he had seen in books. The scribe had found a courtyard in the shade and asked Owen to provide him with additional instruction in swordsmanship.

Thomas advanced again and the Welshman easily turned defence into attack. The young Englishman nearly lost his footing, again – and nearly let out a blasphemous curse that any soldier would have been proud of. The lesson he had learned today was that one cannot always learn things from books.

The two men decided to take a break. Thomas almost wheezed rather than breathed.

"Am I progressing?" the student asked, in hope more than expectation, after catching his breath.

"Well you're not getting any worse," Owen replied.

"Then that's progress."

They both smiled, although Owen was mindful of how worried the youth must have been. The strain on his once cherubic features was clear. The bowman endeavoured to reassure his companion that all would be well.

"I know things may seem, or be, hellish now lad – but one day you will look back on these times and laugh. When we get back home you should come and visit my village. Welsh lamb is the best in all Christendom. As to our women though it's often the case of mutton dressing up as mutton. I'm even looking forward to the rain. I thought the Welsh valleys could be inhospitable, before I came here. So, what are you looking forward to going back to?"

Thomas mentioned that he was looking forward to sampling his mother's cooking once more, getting back to his library and studies – and that he might even write a chronicle of his time on campaign. "I also promised my father before I left that, in return for funding my pilgrimage, I would take over more duties in administering to our family business."

The scribe mustered as much fondness and enthusiasm for his home as he could when speaking, but one of the few things left which Thomas had any faith in was that he would never see his village again.

Edward entered the courtyard. He shared his countryman's faith in the belief that it was unlikely Thomas would make it back to England, especially if he participated in the forthcoming battle. The scribe may have recently killed a man, but he was no killer or soldier. When Thomas first told the knight that he was intending join the mass of pilgrims willing to fight, Edward was tempted to forbid him from doing so. But he wasn't the youth's father. As much as Edward was fearful for Thomas, he also admired his decision. In some ways he was being braver than any trained soldier, for willing to enter the fray.

"You need every fighting man you can get your hands on – and some men who can't fight either," Thomas had half-joked.

Edward issued a few instructions to Owen. The archer had been charged with training a group of pilgrims with some experience with a bow. "The nobles are suddenly grateful for poachers, it seems," the Welshman said with a smile, before taking his leave.

The knight then turned his attention to the scribe.

"I hope you're now an accomplished swordsman, Thomas – as class has ended for the day. We've been summoned by Bohemond. It's unlikely to be good news."

Bohemond warmly welcomed the Englishmen into the dining chamber and poured them some wine. He even deigned to do so himself, instead of ordering an attendant to serve his guests. The prince was in surprisingly good spirits. He had also trimmed his beard – and eyebrows – and wore a freshly laundered surcoat, with a newly daubed cross on the shoulder. Rumour had it that Bohemond had commissioned an artist to paint his portrait. He no longer seemed like a cornered animal. More so he was a prowling tiger, ready to pounce.

Edward soon eyed the plates of food on the table instead of his host. It was a veritable feast. Edward was worried. The bigger the banquet, the more Bohemond would ask of the knight, he judged. A chill ran down his spine and the hairs on the back of his neck pricked up, sensing danger.

"We are celebrating some good news," Bohemond ebulliently announced, wiping the wine from his lips with the back of his hand. "Raymond's condition has worsened. He is bed-ridden, as feverish as a leper with the plague. Let him drown in a pool of sweat. Perhaps God sent the malady, to help narrow our odds of defeating the infidels. He will not, or cannot, contest the Council of Prince's decision to appoint myself to lead our army out against the enemy."

Before being struck down by illness Raymond had been outmanoeuvred by his rival. Bohemond successfully lobbied his fellow noblemen – offering them rewards or denigrating Raymond's leadership – before the key meeting. The Norman put himself forward to command the crusader forces but, echoing Raymond's sentiments in the past, he stated that he would abide by the majority view of the council. He decisively won the vote. Raymond thumped his fist on the table, knocking over his own winecup from the tremor. His voice thundered – calling upon God to curse those who had betrayed him – and he stormed out of the chamber.

Raymond had barely been seen since. Adhemar had told Edward that, instead of being ill, the Frank had been sulking, "Achilles-like," at his billet. As much as the bishop felt sympathy for his old friend, he knew that they had a greater chance of victory with Bohemond - who was more "Odysseus-like" – commanding their forces.

Bohemond went on to explain that he would ask Adhemar to bear the Holy Lance – and that other preparations were meeting expectations. Thankfully the Norman had an eye for logistics, as well as glory. Rations were pooled and prioritised for combatants, which encouraged some to join the army. New recruits were given the requisite basic training and equipment.

Despite various protestations, which Adhemar heard but ultimately dismissed, Bohemond appropriated the provisions and horses of the clergy. When they realised that they were fighting a losing battle to defy Bohemond their bitterness miraculously turned into self-aggrandisement. Priests regularly mentioned in their sermons how they were sacrificing their worldly possessions for the greater good of the campaign – and that congregants, inspired by their example, should do the same for the greater good.

Edward and Thomas listened with intent and the knight nodded with gratitude when Bohemond expressed his thanks for the work the Englishman had carried out in drilling parts of his army. Just as Edward had started to forget about any ulterior motive the Norman might have, just as he ate another piece of salted goat and forgot about how hungry he was, just as the wine he drank began to work its magic, Bohemond changed the subject.

"As you know Edward our main force will depart out of the Bridge Gate when we come to give battle. Kerbogha's personal camp is within sight and reach of the gate. Our objective is to rout our enemy, turn them on their heels, before they can fully mobilise themselves. We have been able to capture a few prisoners over the past few weeks. I would usually trust a Turk as much as I would a priest, but I have received similar intelligence from different sources. Kerbogha understandably keeps his treasury close by to him. I can provide you with some directions and a few troops to support you. Should the opportunity arise, I want you to secure Kerbogha's treasury. Kerbogha may understandably be fond of his wealth and may not wish to abandon it. Should you encounter the enemy general you have my permission to kill him. He will appear less dreadful to people as a corpse, I warrant. He will also find it more difficult to rally his troops if dead."

Thomas' stomach began to churn with fear as it dawned upon him why he had been summoned. He glanced at his countryman but found little solace from doing so. Edward stood with his mouth slightly agape. But any words of defiance failed to issue forth.

"You may need to question the enemy when you enter the camp, which is why Thomas will accompany you."

Bohemond briefly considered how, a year ago, he would have recruited his nephew for the honour, or act of larceny. But Tancred couldn't now be trusted. He was a skilled and redoubtable fighter - but possessed the loyalty of a courtesan. Bohemond would duly reward Edward if he proved successful in his mission. Kerbogha's treasury would not go to waste. It was unlikely that the Norman would be able to secure Constantinople through arms alone. Bohemond considered it ironic that Alexios had usurped the crown through a military coup, as he would lose it through a military coup also. Turkish gold would purchase Greek support. The Byzantine court surrounding Alexios was born for treachery, as a shark is born swimming. It could be bought, like a backstreet whore.

"I know that the idea of victory may seem somewhat fanciful at present. But have faith, my friends. I want you to remember though that some amongst us posited that we could never take Nicaea. Some judged that we would not survive crossing the desert, that we could not triumph at the Battle of Dorylaeum or take possession of this city. I just hope that those self-same doubters are predicting that we cannot prove victorious on the plains of Antioch," Bohemond argued, his eyes gleaming like polished gemstones as he uttered various lines he had rehearsed.

Edward thought how he had been right to be worried earlier and downed another measure of wine, like it would be his last.

16.

The following evening Adhemar invited Edward to dinner. He found the Englishman's company comforting for some reason, as well as entertaining. Although the bishop had a lot on is mind, he didn't want to dwell on things too much. Both men knew that they could be sharing their last supper together. Tomorrow, they could die in battle, as easily as a bough breaking in the wind.

Adhemar coughed again, holding a silk handkerchief up to his mouth. Edward noted that at least his friend wasn't coughing up blood, yet. Thank God for small mercies. The knight welcomed the company too. He had spent a tiring day training new recruits. Their spirit was willing, but their bodies were weak. Some asked the veteran what they should expect in the heat of battle. He was tempted to answer "death". Edward couldn't recall what he actually said. He just knew that his response wasn't particularly useful or inspirational.

His host poured him a cup of fragrant wine.

"This is a special wine, rarer than dragon's milk according to the zealous vintner, which I've been saving for a special occasion. I stole the vintage from Urban's cellar, before departing. I am not without sin, Edward."

The Englishman gulped down the fine vintage in one, although he still savoured the rich taste in his own way, after holding the silver goblet up in a toast to his host beforehand.

"God bless you for your sins," the soldier replied, licking his lips. Not wishing to waste a single drop. Again, like yesternight, Edward appreciated the fine vintage as if it would be the last measure he would ever imbibe.

"All this time, I have been nagging you, more than a wife would her husband, that I should act as your confessor. But the truth is, you have been mine," Adhemar remarked, forcing a smile - which was still nevertheless strained, as he tried to convey that he was well. "As you probably know already, Bohemond has asked me to lead our forces out tomorrow, carrying the Holy Lance as if it were a magic wand. Am I supposed to be honoured? If feels like more of a penance or humiliation. A thought came to me this afternoon, like a revelation. I think Peter Bartholomew found, or planted, a large, mishappen roofer's nail. I am to be a symbol – worshipping a rusty roofer's nail – giving hope and inspiration. I would rather give battle. Perhaps Raymond de Aguilers has already composed some lines involving me dying tomorrow, for his chronicle. I am to be saint and martyr. Urban might not sanction any such proposal, however, once he realises that I liberated one of his finest vintages from the Vatican cellars. I warrant that I would be the patron saint of hypocrites, given that I will be bearing the Holy Lance. Even for a priest, I am to be a paradigm of hypocrisy. But I am not just speaking about my part in the discovery of the relic – my audible silence. Was I not a fraud too at the beginning of the campaign? I was a leading player in the piece of pantomime at Clermont. My taking of the cross was declared as an act of divine inspiration or spontaneity. But I drafted my lines with Urban beforehand, like a playwright needing to deliver a script to a theatre owner. Raymond was in on the act too. Augustus Caesar was perspicacious on his deathbed. "Have I played my part well? Then applaud as I exit," he remarked. We are all actors, playing a part for ourselves or others. Some of us are just more convincing performers. What if I had not pledged to take the cross on that day? Many others may not have committed the cause. Their lives and souls may have been spared. I was responsible for managing Urban's tour in spreading the word about the crusades. I composed many of his sermons and encouraged the crowds, promising wine and salvation."

Edward considered how they were one in the same for him.

"Words are all I can offer, it seems," Adhemar added. "But we need deeds not words. I spent the day preaching, in one form or another. But my words are as empty as my wine cellar. Many pilgrims asked me to bless them today. They asked if we would prove victorious, if God was still on our side. "God will not abandon us, so long as we do not abandon

Him," I sententiously responded. I cursed myself for sounding like Peter the Hermit. But perhaps I am fated to be conceited and vain-glorious, I did after all once desire to be a poet."

Adhemar underwent another brief coughing fit and buried his head in his hands. The despairing, diminished figure before him was in stark contrast to the warrior-bishop he had first encountered. Edward had witnessed Adhemar give sermons in the distance but was usually blissfully unaware of what the bishop was jabbering on about. He did hear Adhemar once preach how the pilgrims were close to God and death, equating the two in order to ease the tormented souls in his congregation.

The two men came face to face in earnest at the Battle of Dorylaeum. Bohemond and his disciplined army had held their formation and staunchly fended off the enemy army, commanded by Kilij Arslan, for a gruelling day. Victory came however when Raymond of Toulouse's army joined the fray and Adhemar, leading a group of knights, outflanked Arslan's formation and turned the tide. A melee ensued. Armies merged. Edward disarmed a Turk about to blindside the skilled and courageous clergyman – by hacking off part of the enemy soldier's limb, below his elbow. Adhemar returned the favour by thrusting his sword into the neck of a wailing opponent, about to blindside the English knight. A mutual nod of thanks turned into an evening of sharing a jug of wine.

Adhemar was one of the few people the misanthropic knight genuinely admired. He wanted to point out to his friend that, should the bishop not have taken up the cross, far more souls would have perished. The leading crusaders would have abandoned the cause or turned on each other. The relationship with Tatikios, Alexios and the support of the Byzantine Empire would have ended before beginning. The Battle of Dorylaeum would have been their final battle. Bohemond would not have been permitted to carry out his plan to infiltrate the city – and they would have been slaughtered on the plains of Antioch. The supply lines from Cyprus that Adhemar established and maintained would have been a mere dream.

When the Englishman entered the bishop's private chambers earlier, he caught him on his knees, devoutly kissing a wooden crucifix.

"Praying for a miracle?" Edward asked, as his friend rose to greet him.

"Bohemond is confident that we are not in need of one. Or he believes he is the miracle, God's gift to the crusade," Adhemar replied. His dry cough hadn't completely snuffed out his dry wit, Edward was pleased to note.

The taciturn knight didn't quite know what to say as his friend sat with his head in his hands, exasperated and exhausted. As a mangonel can launch stone after stone and chip away at the most steadfast of walls, so too had the campaign chipped away at his friend's faith and constitution.

Edward was thankfully saved from any prolonged awkwardness by an intervention from Rainald. The attendant entered and asked his master if he would like anything, before the rest of the staff retired for the evening.

"I will be fine. And thank you for the meal too," Adhemar warmly remarked, not wishing to pass on the malady of his despondency to his household. Rainald had trapped a few swallows earlier, which the bishop and knight had eaten, by strategically tying some fishhooks around the dome of the cathedral, where some of the birds nested.

Rainald took his leave and Adhemar endured another bout of coughing. His face reddened to the colour of his wine almost, Edward observed, before the Englishman refilled his friend's cup of water.

"Thank you. You should be careful in coming too close. I might be contagious."

"Dying in agony from a virulent disease is the least of my concerns at the moment," Edward wryly replied.

Adhemar emitted a cough cum laugh.

"I admire your ability to find flashes of humour in the darkest of hours Edward," the bishop said, recalling a verse from the Bible. *Being cheerful keeps you healthy. It is a slow death to be gloomy all the time.*

"It's in the darkest hours when we need humour the most," the Englishman argued. Like we need God, he was going to reply. But desisted.

Campfires dotted the plains of Antioch like shrubs. Emma pulled her cloak around her to trap in the heat – and Edward pulled her close to him. The couple, surveying the landscape from the battlements, could also make out tents, spectral figures and the dull glint of blades.

By the end of tomorrow the scene would be markedly different, the knight mused. Eviscerated bodies would litter the scene like weeds. The defeated might be piled up, their limbs entangled, and be burning like campfires. Screams would stain the air, as the victors turned the wounded into corpses. The familiar tang of blood, horse dung and the beginnings of bodily decay would worm their way into his nostrils. If he was still alive, instead of part of a funeral pyre.

Emma heard a low, murmuring drone emanate from the enemy camp, spreading across it like a film of oil covering a pool of water. The Muslims were chanting. One religion of peace was doubtless praying for the death and destruction of another. When the Antiochenes occupied the walls, could they hear the pilgrims praying? More so the odd bout of singing could be heard from the crusader camp, accompanied by bawdy jokes and laughter. Emma thought it a little strange – and a little sad – that she couldn't hear any laughter or music ring out from the enemy. If their prayers were set to music, it would resemble a dirge.

Edward narrowed his gaze and tried to make out the wending course of the Orontes. Or the river Styx, as Thomas had called it earlier.

"They do not seem particularly happy, or at peace," she commented, leaning into Edward.

"They're only human too," he replied.

"Tonight may be the night that Thomas proves that he's only human as well. Herleva mentioned that she's intending to spend the evening with him. She's with him now, I imagine."

The knight widened his eyes in pleasant surprise.

"Some sins of the flesh will do him the world of good. Perhaps there are such things as miracles after all. Alas, he probably doesn't know what to do with it."

"Thankfully Herleva knows what to do with it, for the both of them."

"I just hope that she doesn't wear him out too much. I want him to be saddle sore and bowlegged after having ridden a warhorse, not before."

"I'm more worried about you. You won't do anything foolish tomorrow, will you?" Emma asked, moving her head in order to gauge Edward's aspect as he answered.

"I can't promise anything. We seem to be living in an age of foolishness. Although perhaps all eras are ages of foolishness. Folly is a plague – and there doesn't appear to be a cure," the knight offered up. He refrained from telling Emma about the mission Bohemond had charged him with. But he hadn't told Bohemond that he had little intention of fulfilling his mission. It would be one too many suicide missions, Edward concluded.

I want to live. For her.

Their bed in his small room was now the centre of the world. Not Jerusalem. The night was far from balmy, but their bodies were covered with a film of sweat.

She made him forget about hunger pangs and stomach cramps. She caused the images of scimitar-wielding, ululating enemies rushing towards him, to disappear. Vanquishing them. Guilt and God no longer haunted him, as regular as the sound of church bells. It would also have been discourteous, at the very least, to think about Yeva when he was being intimate with Herleva.

As he lay in bed, thinking about earlier in the evening, Thomas couldn't recall what he was talking about when Herleva stopped his mouth with a kiss, as she squeezed his clammy palm and pulled him closer. It didn't matter what he was talking about, he realised. Desire was sprinkled throughout the room like motes of dust, shimmering in the candlelight. He liked the way her lips tasted of wine and her fading perfume was manna compared to Antioch's other deleterious odours. Something awakened inside him. He felt a little possessed. Or he was in possession of a new feeling, which he yearned to break in like a knight would a fresh horse. She managed to unbutton her linen dress without looking. He briefly thought about what his mother might say to him, for giving into the temptations of the flesh. But his mother was the last person he wanted to imagine.

"Trust me," she whispered, tenderly yet commandingly, before kissing and sucking his earlobe. The scribe hadn't felt anything resembling the sensation before. Herleva sometimes told Thomas where to kiss her, touch her, and he studiously obeyed. They may only have one night together. She wanted it to be memorable, for both of them. He babbled a few things, like he was speaking in tongues, when she guided him inside of her. He was shy, gentle – but then more passionate. She wanted to make him as happy as he made her. The experienced whore felt like a young woman again, capable of sweetness and devotion. Thomas couldn't be sure, but he thought at one moment, as Herleva tossed her head back and climaxed, that she said she loved him. Only partly because he couldn't be sure if she uttered the words, Thomas didn't say anything back. Yet at that moment he was as devoted to the whore as any knight was to any maiden in any poem. He would have held his hand over the burning brazier in the corner for her. She just needed to order him to do so.

During their second bout of lovemaking Herleva straddled him. He was surprised by her strength, as her slender, sinewy legs held him in place – pinning him down, like a wolf about to devour its prey. He didn't mind.

Thomas finally caught his breath, although his heart still galloped. Herleva lay beside him - similarly glowing inside and out. Usually she felt unfulfilled after sex. Although she pretended otherwise to some clients, it was a business transaction. She liked making money above making love. She was glad when she tired men out and then they fell asleep, if they paid for her for an entire evening. But Herleva wanted neither of them to fall asleep now. Seeing him content made her content. But there was no knowing how much time they had left together. Or there was, unfortunately.

He wondered whether he should tell Edward and Owen about his night with Herleva. Would he be impinging upon her honour, or boasting? What with bedding a woman and taking part in a battle, he could now consider himself a man. Even if he would only do so for a day. His thoughts suddenly became tinged with doubt and melancholy when he thought that Herleva might only have been intimate with him from an act of charity. She may have understandably believed that she would never see him again. Thomas imagined, before she kissed him, that she would ask for money in exchange with having sex with him. He also imagined himself, desperate and desirous, agreeing to any proposal and fee.

As Herleva slotted her supple body even closer to his – and she gazed at him, beaming, he realised that her expression wasn't shaped by pity. Perhaps she had declared that she loved him earlier – and meant it. Thomas didn't quite know what to conclude. The scholar needed to time think. Dissect.

"Could you compose a poem for me?" Herleva asked, her voice gleaming, mindful of not saying that she wanted something to remember him by. She had already openly cursed Bohemond's name to Emma for ordering the scribe to serve as a soldier.

"I would love to. You inspire me," Thomas replied, with a modicum of charm and amorousness – which was a first for him. He closed his eyes briefly, but rather than reaching into his imagination, Thomas delved into his memory and adapted a poem he had written for Yeva. He threw in a few lines from the *Song of Solomon* for good measure. Herleva yearned to kiss the young Englishman, but that would have stemmed the flow of beautiful words.

"Your hair is beautiful upon your cheeks and falls along your neck like jewels… The day is a but a shadow of a day without seeing the empyreal light in her eyes… To feel her kiss is to be touched by God, or at least a goddess… Like a lily among thorns is my darling among women."

Any discomfort and guilt Thomas experienced at pretending to have composed the poem spontaneously was forgotten as the whore disappeared below the blanket and did things that he couldn't possibly commit to verse - or tell his mother about.

17.

The sky wasn't quite pitch black, but it was a deep purple when Thomas woke. Different parts of his body ached, in different ways, to what he was used to – yet any aches were a price worth paying, he judged. Thomas was careful not to cause Herleva to stir. As much as part of him wanted to wake her, he didn't want to disturb her peaceful slumber. Nor did he want her to remember him as being so morose and scared. His hands trembled, not from any chill in the air, as he dressed. Thomas wanted Herleva to remember him at his best.

The newly drafted soldier proceeded to travel to a former market square in the city, where a large contingent of Bohemond's company were assembling. Owen had sharpened his sword for him, the day before. Edward had given his countryman a helm and hauberk. He may have looked like a knight, but he certainly didn't feel like one. A fair few other pilgrims mustering in the square appeared equally out of place. Seasoned soldiers were nervous too, knowing what might befall them on the other side of the Bridge Gate. They had given battle before against superior-sized forces, but their current odds of victory or survival were about as long as the walls of Antioch, should they be rolled out like a carpet. Or as long as the length of the Euphrates. The waiting was unbearable, but not as unbearable as what could follow. Senior knights barked out instructions. Horses whinnied in the background. Birds trilled too, confused or irate at having been disturbed. Thomas also occasionally heard puking noises, sometimes creating a domino effect. Words of sympathy rather than abuse were offered up.

Dawn began to stretch its limbs and the horizon glowed like the ends of a pair of blacksmith's tongs.

Thomas had initially been enthralled by the idea of being part of history, when they first set off on the pilgrimage. He could have never imagined that he would be forming up to give battle, however. On another day it might have bolstered his heart or pride. But right now, the best he could do was prevent himself from sobbing or retching. He craved some wine, to help fortify his spirits. He would have liked it if Edward and Owen could be with him. But he knew that his friends had to be elsewhere. Drawing first blood.

A path to the battlefield needed to be opened-up, by ploughing through the enemy camp of soldiers occupying the stone bridge which sat between the city and the plains of Antioch. Bohemond decided to send out a contingent of archers to attack the Turks – supported by Hugh de Vermandois and his company of mounted knights.

The younger brother of Philip I, the French king, the Count of Vermandois was eager to make a name for himself during the campaign. Today was the day to do so, Bohemond believed. The nobleman could be pompous and vain (traits not altogether uncommon among the nobility). He employed both a blacksmith and barber in his retinue. Rumour had it that he dyed the grey in his beard - and he insisted that he should be referred to as Hugh the Great. Few shared the high opinion he had of himself. But his troops were not without ability. Hugh could be bold, bordering on reckless, but Bohemond welcomed such a mindset for the present assignment. He encouraged the French prince by arguing that, although he did not eclipse his brother in rank, he could in glory.

The order was given to unbar the gate. A gaggle of priests surrounded the force, uttering prayers and flicking holy water. As an army of squinting eyes attached themselves to Bohemond, mounted on a fine black destrier, he willed himself to appear confident and calm. Some young, fearful soldiers looked how he felt, but the general dared not show it. He offered up a few words to put some iron in their souls – and help distract himself.

"My brothers. Most men only get to be spectators when it comes to history. Today, we get to make it. Christendom will herald our deeds, for as long as there is a Christendom. Christ and St Andrew are with us. The Holy Lance may be our spearpoint, but we must drive it home. We are armoured with faith and a just cause. You are fighting for God – and for the stout-hearted pilgrims fighting alongside you. You are also fighting for your father, son or brother working your lands back home. For do you think that the infidel will stop at the conquest of Antioch? We may be the first and last line of defence between the bestial heathen and our womenfolk... We have bested the Turk before. We can and will do so again. They may outnumber us, but they cannot outfight us."

War cries were consciously suppressed as the archers swarmed through the Bridge Gate and fanned out. They wished to remain as quiet as the flight of an arrow, so as not to alert the enemy to their surprise attack.

Hugh de Vermandois, mounted on a lean chestnut charger, positioned himself between the two blocks of bowmen, his arm held aloft. Jaw thrust forward. Waiting for his men to assemble and nock their arrows. The deadlier their first coordinated volley was, the better.

Bohemond had requested (and the prince's requests were tantamount to orders) than any knights accomplished with a bow should join the vanguard of troops tasked with capturing the bridge and routing the enemy there. Although Edward wasn't in the class of archer as Owen, he decided to volunteer. He wanted to fight alongside his friend, even if it might be for the last time.

The Englishman nocked his arrow. A bed of sweat ran down his temple and was threatening to curve into the corner of his eye but he ignored it. Hugh de Vermandois turned to both groups of archers and nodded his head. Dozens and dozens of pilgrims drew their bowstrings back. The old wound in the knight's shoulder ached again. But the discomfort was worth it. He was about to kill the enemy.

A smattering of Turks, rubbing sleep out of their eyes, on and around the bridge, noticed the enemy forming up. Some hearts momentarily stopped. Some pounded like the hooves of the Four Horsemen. They sounded the alarm and bellowed out conflicting orders. But it was too little, too late.

Arrows shot through the air like a brood of hornets, but with far deadlier stings. They pierced armour, eyeballs, mouths, throats. Whooshing and thudding sounds were legion, although some of the missiles clattered against the stone bridge. Bodies twisted and fell, to a chorus of teeth-itching screams.

Volley succeeded volley. Owen offered advice and encouragement to the band of new recruits he had recently helped to train.

"Pierre, pull back on your bowstring and aim a touch higher. Wasting an arrow is as cardinal a sin as wasting a drink... Odo, you don't know your own strength. You're overshooting. Your arrows are landing closer to Jerusalem than Antioch."

Fire arrows arced across the roseate dawn and started to set tents alight, fuelling the panic. A small contingent of crossbowmen had joined the vanguard. But Owen had emptied half his cloth bag full of arrows before any of the auxiliaries had a chance to unleash a second quarrel.

The archers delivered death and disarray. The enemy were moving off the bridge, showing the crusaders their backs. It was time to finish off those taking cover or showing resistance. Hugh gave the order for his knights to advance. Some drew swords. Some couched their lances.

A trot turned into a canter, which turned into a gallop. The archers concentrated their aim on those retreating, on the far side of the bridge, so as not to accidentally hit their comrades. The Count of Vermandois' usually sharp, supercilious features were contorted in rage as he swung his broadsword and made his first kill. The point of his sharpened weapon then stabbed down into the terrified face of a second foe. When he wheeled his horse around the hind of the creature knocked another assailant to the ground. The Turk's head cracked open like an egg as it struck the stone bridge. The knights in the nobleman's company bloodied their blades too and hacked the enemy down, as if for sport.

Bohemond surveyed the scene with satisfaction. If he owned an inclination to pray, the Norman would have asked God that the routing of the Muslims on the bridge might prove a sign of things to come. There was a resolute lack of resolve among some of the Turkish troops. But there was no time to pray. Deeds, not words, mattered.

Some might have considered that the Army of God resembled the army of the damned as Bohemond issued the order for the various companies to exit the city through the Bridge Gate and form up on the plains of Antioch.

The first to march out was a contingent of French troops, under the command of Robert of Flanders. Some of the combatants were a little bedraggled but beneath their besmirched weeds and unkempt beards were seasoned fighters. They were willing and able to kill. Bohemond was encouraged by the eager gait of the troops. They were lifting their feet instead of dragging them.

Conrad was conspicuous by his absence as Godfrey led off his army of Lotharingians. The prince had mourned his lieutenant like a brother. Many pilgrims attended the funeral service, believing that wine and victuals might be provided after the ceremony. Like Edward, Godfrey had vowed to cut down the dishonourable infidel should he encounter Radwan on the battlefield. As Godfrey passed by Bohemond, he offered his fellow prince a nod of respect. Within the nod of respect was a nod of gratitude, as the Norman had lent Godfrey a suitably handsome mount, after his own had recently perished. Horses were, alas, too few and far between. The majority of knights were reduced – traduced, some might have argued – to fighting on foot. Some were choosing to ride pack animals. The spectacle of a haughty Count Hartmann of Dillingen riding a braying, gap-toothed donkey would have ordinarily been a source of amusement. But no one was currently laughing.

A force of Normans, let by Robert of Normandy, followed. The commander and his soldiers were a picture of grim determination. Bohemond preferred the look to one of a lack of determination. When Hugh de Vermandois had asked about the number of combatants the crusaders could field and if it would prove sufficient for them to prevail, Robert of Normandy had answered for Bohemond.

"It will have to be."

Bohemond wryly smiled to himself as he witnessed the Bishop of Le Puy lead out Raymond's forces of Toulousians and Provencals. He was wearing armour rather than a cassock - and wielding a sword rather than the Holy Lance. The relic was being carried by Raymond of Aguilers, who rode next to him. Adhemar could be as wily as his own father, Bohemond thought to himself, with a sense of admiration rather than opprobrium. The bishop had informed Raymond of Toulouse that he had been instructed by the Norman that he should bear the Holy Lance into battle. Ever willing to challenge and thwart his rival, the Count of Toulouse, who judged himself the custodian of the relic, gave the order for his chaplain Raymond of Aguilers to carry the weapon. The chronicler made notes as he rode out. He would have quite a story to tell, if he lived to tell it. Whether Adhemar had feigned disappointment or not, he was doubtless relieved to be free from carrying – and tacitly endorsing – the lance. But the bishop was not the only crusader capable of guile. Bohemond had paid a handful of knights in his rival's company to remain close to Adhemar and provide him with some mortal protection. If the Norman prince could have anyone survive this day, aside from himself, it would be the bishop. Adhemar had kept the disparate collection of princes together before Antioch. They would similarly need his unifying presence after the battle, even if it meant Bohemond possessing less influence as a result

The bulk of new recruits generated by the discovery of the lance had attached themselves to Raymond's army, swelling its ranks. Interspersed with knights and men-at-arms were groups of unarmoured pilgrims, carrying billhooks, clubs and mallets. There had been an increase in the past few days in the demand for clergymen to administer communion and take confessions. Some Christians fasted and purified themselves. Bohemond hoped that the new troops weren't ready to meet their maker quite yet. Certainly, many of them had something to fight for, as he noticed how plenty of womenfolk came out to see their husbands and sons off. They tried – but failed miserably – to hold back their tears.

Tancred's squad of knights passed by next. Bohemond recognised soldiers who had once served him, but he judged that their loyalty was now to his nephew. Although young, Tancred was a seasoned warrior, who had earned the respect of his men. He dauntlessly rode at the head of every cavalry charge. Even as a boy his nephew wished to be first in everything. But so did Bohemond. Bohemond had often received complaints about his arrogant, young kinsman, when Tancred first served in his army. But the adolescent nobleman was often contemptuous of those deserving of contempt. Perhaps Bohemond should've censured the upstart more in his formative years. For it was too late now. Bohemond had recently tried to temper his nephew's pursuit of more wealth and power.

"Be mindful not to be too ambitious, Tancred, lest your reach exceeds your grasp."

"I am not sure I can hear you properly, over the sound of irony. I am my own man now uncle, partly because you taught me well."

Aye, too well, Bohemond mused. Despite his questionable loyalty however, Tancred would know who the enemy was today. His nephew would cut down more Turks than most – and he hoped they would be able to share some battle stories, over a jug of wine, before nightfall. Bohemond realised that he missed conspiring with his nephew. He had shared his plans with his kinsman, concerning securing Antioch as a prize and one day capturing Constantinople. But increasingly Tancred nurtured his own plans and ambitions. Bohemond noticed how his nephew grew rightly distrustful of the Byzantines, after Alexios swooped in like a harpy to steal Nicaea from the crusaders. Baldwin's betrayal festered in Tancred's soul too. His loyalty was solely to himself, even if he recently aligned himself with Raymond. The boy may one day eclipse my fame, Bohemond conceded.

But just let it be after my death.

Bohemond's own army was the last to file out of the Bridge Gate. They marched in good order. The likes of Edward and Fulk of Chartres had drilled the men well. His troops would initially act as a reserve force to support other contingents, in case Kerbogha launched an attack while the crusaders formed up on the plains. From the lack of numbers posted on the bridge – and due to the fact that the enemy were still heavily dispersed around the entire city – Bohemond was confident that Kerbogha was unsuspecting and ill-prepared for their attack.

The crusaders, armoured and coated in dust, were fanned out across the plains, ready to give battle. If war was akin to a game of chess, it was his opponent's move, Bohemond mused.

18.

The emirs present scrunched up their faces, in confusion or concern. Kerbogha's hand, clutching a pawn in his fingertips, remained in mid-air as Watthab ibn Mahmud, an Arab commander, rushed into the tent – his scabbard slapping against his thigh, his earrings and necklaces jingling. Mahmud was a stolid, stout-hearted soldier. But he was clearly perturbed. Sweat drenched his burnished features.

"The westerners have left the city. They are forming up to give battle, by the bridge. I have seen it with my own eyes, as much as I can scarce believe it still. Ahmad Marwan has raised his black flag above the citadel. Should we give him the countersignal to advance? The city must be largely undefended. Should I start to form up our forces?" Mahmud breathlessly asked, his fringe of black hair matted to his forehead. Initially, when one of his men alerted him to the infidels streaming out of the gate, the Arab believed that the enemy were attempting to flee.

"There is no need to panic. The day will be ours. Allah wills it. This move by the desperate pilgrims is not unexpected," Kerbogha calmly remarked, lying. He did not want to give any satisfaction to the emirs, or display any weakness, by conceding that he had been outwitted by the enemy. He cursed the son of Robert Guiscard under his breath, however. "Give the order for our armies to form up, but do not instruct them to attack. I do not want to force half of the heathens back into the city. This is our chance to defeat them with one, swift killing stroke. If they retreat behind the city walls once more, the siege will continue. As to Marwan, signal him to hold his position. We are unaware of the strength of numbers inside Antioch. I also do not wish to allow Ahmad's men to pillage the city, depriving our own troops of any spoils."

Kerbogha also had no desire to share the glory of his triumph. It had long been his intention to be the first man to enter the city and claim it as his prize. He had already composed some lines for when his scribe would record the event. The victory would be his own – and Allah's. The self-interested, snivelling emirs lacked vision. This battle would not be the end of things, but a beginning. His army would sweep across the land like the Prophet's once did. Aleppo and Constantinople would fall. There would be a blood price – there always is – but Kerbogha judged that he would bring peace to the region. The emirs needed to show more faith. Things were going to plan. If only he had been able to force the ignoble Baldwin out into the open, instead of cowering behind his walls at Edessa. His allies were ingrates, behaving like a wife complaining that her garden is too large, or she has too many slaves to service her every whim. They should be honouring him, for creating such a grand army and provisioning it so successfully.

"I will send the necessary message to the citadel. What of the orders for other forces?" Watthab Mahmud asked, outwardly loyal and obedient.

"In the same way that we encircled the city, we will surround their paltry, enfeebled army. Bring the troops up from the gates of St Paul and St George. They are not to engage the enemy until commanded to do so, however. The infidels may well surrender or attempt to retreat, once they confront their fate, and we will avoid a significant clash of arms," Kerbogha pronounced, before completing his chess move. He would finish his game – and deign to start another – rather than being harried into dealing with the vermin. Perhaps Bohemond and Raymond of Toulouse were posturing – and aiming to negotiate. Kerbogha recalled his encounter with Shams ad-Daulah. The conceited son of Yaghi Siyan had postured too, believing he was in a position to negotiate over the control of the stronghold.

"You can either give me the citadel, or I will take it from you," Kerbogha proposed, with more than a little indignation in his voice, ending the negotiations before they started. He would present a similar ultimatum to the westerners, should they wish to negotiate over the ownership of Antioch.

Mahmud bowed his head in compliance as Kerbogha gave further orders for various emirs to place their armies in the front ranks, whilst the bulk of his own forces would support them.

"Go to your men. Put fire in the bellies of your soldiers. This is what we have all been waiting for. We will soon have the infidels in the palm of our hands. We need only squeeze, to ground them into dust," Kerbogha asserted, as he held his hand aloft and balled it into a fist. The general was slightly distracted whilst he spoke, however, as an increasing cacophony of noise could be heard from outside the tent. Word was spreading of the enemy's advance, as was a sense of alarm.

"I have left my sword and shield on the other side of the camp," one voice bemoaned. "Tell the imams to pray for us," another shrilly instructed.

Kerbogha scowled. Radwan had previously warned him that indiscipline was creeping into the army. It was up to the emirs and commanders to drill their troops, to sharpen them like a blade. Too many of the emirs were more concerned with stuffing their faces or gossiping about their mistresses, rather than diligently training their armies.

Radwan similarly appeared like he was about to breathe fire. He harrumphed, with his arms folded across his broad, heaving chest. As much as he was irritated by the wretches outside, he was annoyed at himself and the westerners. He had expected the curs to curl up and die, like leaves in autumn. For once, Radwan was also annoyed at his master. He knew that Kerbogha was lying when he pronounced that he had expected the attack. But the loyal lieutenant would keep the truth to himself.

"Are they in possession of the Holy Lance, Watthab?" Matar of Harran asked, curious or fearful, coughing afterwards as dust filled the tent from the activity outside. Matar was nearly being put off his food by the impending battle.

Kerbogha shot his supposed ally a baleful look, as he also took in several emirs and senior commanders whispering to one another, conspiratorially.

Emma bribed an invalided man-at-arms so that she and Herleva could stand on the walls and watch the battle unfold. The various crusader contingents had merged into one army, spread out across the plain. Emma thought to herself how she had never witnessed so many soldiers gathered in one place, until she witnessed the enemy troops begin to stream out of their camps and knit together. An island of Christians would soon sit within an ocean of Turks and Arabs.

Alongside the colourfully dressed women on the walls stood rows of black-clad, bare-footed clergymen, praying for the brave pilgrims. Some raised their voices to send their Latin phrases into the aether, in competition with one another, like birds chirping in the nest for their mother to feed them. They clutched bibles to their chests, lit candles and held crosses above their heads. They prayed for their fellow Christians, that they might live – and not just because if they lived, it was likely that they would survive too.

A few priests, young and old, covertly glanced at the women of ill-repute, in between closing their eyes to pray. Some knew the prostitutes, or their reputations, and looked askance with a degree of priggishness or perversity in their glassy aspects – either undressing them with their eyes or envisioning the harlots being put in the stocks. There was also a number of chaplains who intentionally averted their gaze away from the striking women, ignoring them – as they had proved regular frequenters of Emma's establishments and they didn't want to betray their familiarity with the whores.

Emma barely gave any of the priests a second look. Her focus was on the souls below. Or one soul. She prayed, for God to spare Edward. She had seldom asked for anything else in her life. Emma thought how she had only really devoutly prayed three times before. The first time was as a young girl, when her father passed away. He was a good man and could be fond of his daughter – and not just when in his cups. Emma had knelt in church and prayed that her father had ascended to Heaven, although later in life she realised that he probably would have preferred the company in Hell. The second time she prayed in earnest was during the first months of working in her profession. A customer, a merchant, turned on the girl and savagely beat her. He pummelled her face and cut her breast and buttocks. As Emma lay in bed, recovering from her injuries, she begged God for the man to be apprehended and face the law. But the law did nothing. The law could be bought, like a whore. When divine justice was found wanting as well, Emma paid another client, in services rather than coin, to deliver retribution. He did. The merchant spent twice the amount of time recovering from his injuries as Emma did from hers. A friend had argued that she had gone too far, but Emma replied that she hadn't gone far enough in punishing the caitiff. The last time her soul had reached out to God had been recently. She had prayed that Edward would survive the night, when he scaled the walls to infiltrate the city and open the George Gate. Emma realised that her life would be less of a life without the gruff but good-hearted Englishman in it. Emma had grown used to only depending upon herself over the years, for fear of being deceived or hurt, but she here prayed to God for Edward, more than she had prayed for anyone else, including herself.

Please spare him, even if you need to sacrifice others to do so. Let a gust of wind blow any arrow off course, aimed at his heart. I love him.

"Do you regret staying here? There was a time when we could have travelled back to Taranto," Herleva asked, her voice mired in future grief, as she tucked a few loose strands of hair blowing in her eyes behind her ear. She could not claim to know much about military matters and soldiering, but she could count. And the enemy outnumbered Bohemond's doomed army. At best she would be sold into slavery. At worst she would be abused and killed by the barbaric infidels. Although the young woman preferred not to think about what some of the Christian soldiers had done to the women of Antioch, she did not believe that the Muslims would behave any differently. There was little reasoning with a man, or appealing to any Godliness, when his blood was up.

"I would distrust anyone who claimed not to have any regrets. I certainly regret some of my hairstyles over the years – and paying for expensive dresses which I only ever wore once or twice. I regret some of the choices of men I let into my bed – although I never regretted overcharging them. Thankfully many of them were memorably forgettable. I also regret asking you about your time with Thomas last night. I am not sure I can ever look upon him again and consider him as sweet and innocent as I once did."

"But do you regret remaining here?" Herleva asked again, for once blushing, as her friend mentioned Thomas.

"No," Emma replied, as she thought of Edward and smiled, wanly.

The enemy advanced, forming and tightening the cordon around the Army of God – like a noose tightening around a condemned man's neck.

19.

The air shimmered in the heat, like ripples in a pond. But still plenty of pilgrims shivered, like dogs left out in the cold. Fear was legion, sewn into every breast like the crosses sewn upon surcoats and tunics. The ground also trembled beneath the Christians' feet as hordes of hostile Muslims moved slowly but inexorably towards them. Thomas thought that if he closed his eyes, he could well imagine he was about to experience an earthquake. But God would not order the plains to crack open and swallow the enemy army up, unfortunately.

Edward stood next to his countryman and scratched his beard beneath his helm. His hauberk weighed heavy, but it would feel lighter once the fighting started. His gambeson soaked up the sweat pouring from his torso. Not for the first time, he wondered if he was taking part in his last battle. Before, his only regret had been that he had never found – and eviscerated – the men who had killed his parents during the Harrying of the North. He realised however that he had a fresh regret, like a fresh wound. He should have asked Adhemar to marry him and Emma. Edward wanted to be with her in this life and the next.

A few horses whinnied. But all too few. Various horns, communicating orders, sounded in the background, lowing like cattle, as the enemy manoeuvred to all but surround the crusaders. A few heads bobbed up and down as soldiers stood on tiptoe, endeavouring to gain a better view of the sight they wished they could unsee. Banners were raised, taunts were traded – although few from either side could understand their counterparts.

Clouds began to congregate on the horizon and similarly moved, slowly but inexorably, towards the crusaders. Edward felt the temperature drop. Damp pervaded the air, as well as fear. It would rain, thank God.

Let the shower soak the bowstrings of the bastards.

Bohemond shared the same thought and the two men glanced at one another, permitting themselves the minutest of smiles. The prince's barrelled chest expanded that little bit more than usual as he addressed his men once more, his stentorian voice even reaching those in the rear ranks.

"We have planted ourselves like great oaks, men. Our roots have plunged deep into the ground. No gust of wind or wave of flimsy arrows can blow us over. The Turks will come and aim to hack us down. But we will not yield. We carry our own blades – and we will be the ones chopping them down, like saplings. Tomorrow we can wake, free to roam inside and outside the city. Tomorrow we can feast on the fruits of victory and wade in the waters of the Orontes. Tomorrow we can march onwards, to Jerusalem. The Mount of Olives and the Holy of Holies still await. But for us to realise that tomorrow we must win today. I have faith that your hearts and sword arms will hold. All you need to do is have faith in yourselves and each other," Bohemond proclaimed. He was going to close with another shout of, "No retreat, no surrender," but he didn't want to repeat himself. The crescendo of cheers and chorus of "God wills it!" would have drowned him out regardless.

"Are you ready?" Edward asked, hoping that he could be heard over the clamour.

Thomas nodded in reply, not knowing if his fiend was referring to being ready to fight or ready to die. He wasn't sure if he was ready for either. But he would have to be.

Edward offered the nervous youth an encouraging smile as he tightened the chin strap on the raw recruit's helmet.

"I'll try and keep an eye on you. Keep an eye on me too. I've also asked others to keep an eye on both of us. Battles can unfold in ways that not even their Prophet can predict. If we can get through this, lad, I'll duly reward you with a jug of wine, no matter how much some bastard overcharges me for it. But that will still pale in comparison to the reward Herleva will give you."

Thomas crimsoned but couldn't help suppress a smile on hearing the girl's name – and remembering the way he had felt yesternight.

"Do you think that she might consider me a knight, after this?"

"Today, we're all knights," Edward replied, without hesitation, as the tall Englishman gazed over the heads of his brethren and surveyed the enemy. Worried yet proud. Bloodthirsty but virtuous.

Watthab Mahmud returned, his face freckled with rain as well as awash with perspiration, to update his commander.

"Have the infidels begun to break and flee yet? Or have they signalled that they wish to negotiate?" Kerbogha asked, as an attendant strapped him into his finely wrought armour.

"The Christians will die before they flee, I believe," Mahmud replied, wishing to dispel his superior of any delusions. The situation was grave. Graver than anything they faced at Edessa. "If all the pagan world rushed against them, they would not budge a foot. They are here to fight, not flee."

Kerbogha briefly pursed his lips. He did not like Arab's tone. There was a hint of insolence in his words. Mahmud seemed to be admiring the spirit of the enemy, whilst delivering the unwelcome news. Kerbogha would demote the officer – and promote his nearest rival – once the battle was over.

The rain fell, as did a shower of arrows from the Muslim army. The noise resembled hundreds of carpenter hammers tapping in nails. But shields were raised – and the storm was weathered. Many knew that they could survive such an awesome attack because they had done so before. Veterans offered encouragement to new recruits and a few soldiers even exchanged jokes beneath the panoply of bucklers.

"This is nothing. You should experience one of my wife's relentless barrages, after I come home late from drinking... I've just bloody remembered. It's pissing raining and I left my washing out. Could this day get any worse?"

God did not need to blow some of the arrows off course, as many spat into the ground or sailed high into the air, landing with all the force of a horse chestnut upon a shield. Most of the conscripts had not kept up their training or maintained their weapons properly – or bothered to exert themselves when pulling their damp bowstrings back.

Arms soon grew tired and the supply of arrows became exhausted. The attack caused few serious injuries and even fewer deaths. The crusaders' hearts and armour had held, for now.

But the day was just beginning. The initial assault was but an appetiser, before the main banquet.

Like a behemoth stirring, a mass of infantry and cavalry advanced against the enemy's left flank, unprotected by the river. But in this game of human chess Bohemond had anticipated his opponent's move. The Norman arranged beforehand for Rainald of Toul – and a force of hardened Lotharingians and Franks – to guard against the flank collapsing.

"The line must be held, which is why I am bidding you to hold it," Bohemond remarked to the Count of Toul the night before. He knew that Rainald had something to prove to his father and also his kinsman, Godfrey of Bouillon. The nobleman was a devout Christian, but not so devout that he would show mercy to their foes. Rainald was fond of reading poetry and tales of chivalrous deeds – but poetry would be the last thing on his mind when he donned his armour. His men would engage the enemy with pride and malice. Bohemond couldn't ask for anything more, or better.

Radwan, appreciating the strategic importance of the attack, offered to lead the army but Kerbogha refused to acquiesce. The general wanted his lieutenant close by, when he led a second wave of men to put down any lingering resistance. He had also already tasked young Asim, a nephew of the Emir of Damascus, to command the detachment. Should he replace the nephew now it would be considered an insult to the family – and the emir might not be beyond standing his army down in protest at the affront to his family's honour.

BESIEGED

The two gnashing armies clashed. A cavalry charge was first deployed by Asim to break through the enemy's line. But Rainald mustered what few mounted knights he could to blunt the force of the attack and the line held. The Count of Toul was a man possessed. Constantly fighting. Constantly rallying his troops. The words of Godfrey also reverberated in the ears of the Lotharingians, after he had inspired them to fight in the name of God – and for the honour of their slain comrade, Conrad. When Rainald lost his sword, he wielded a mace, breaking jaws and smashing eye sockets without, or with, prejudice. A giant sprawl of Muslim infantry advanced and engaged. The line of Rainald's men-at-arms and unmounted knights bowed - but did not break. Blood and bone sprayed through the air like horse spittle. Some in Asim's army wondered why the enemy were not retreating, until they realised that there was no place to retreat to. The soldiers in the middle and rear ranks of the Muslim force could hear the sluicing sounds of blade cutting through flesh. The screams were as high pitched as a eunuch singing. They had little desire to join the fray – and remained safely ensconced in the herd of men. Every weapon was brought to bear by the pilgrims however, as they ferociously battled for their lives and the lives of the comrades next to them. The enemy's dead began to pile up, partly creating a defensive barricade. The Lotharingians continued to hack away and thrust their gore-strewn weapons forwards. Their blood was up. "What the Germans lack in a sense of humour, they make up with a sense of honour," Edward had once explained to Thomas. Asim watched on, aghast. The youth had pictured his army's advance differently, to say the least. A lieutenant asked if he wanted to give the order to keep moving forward or retreat, but Asim couldn't hear the concerned officer over the raucous dirge of battle. His first battle would be his last.

Many Turks fought well. But not well enough. The tide was slowly but perceptibly turning. The ranks of veterans had been thinned – some lay injured, some lay dead – and the conscripts lacked the stomach for the fight. If the Christians had slaughtered their lions, they could easily slaughter their lambs.

Many of the cavalry bolted too. Some would doubtless blame their horses for doing so. Bohemond had given Rainald orders to contain any advance, but the enemy were now turning on their heels. His men were counterattacking out of instinct, rage. Let them, the nobleman thought. Every Muslim they killed now wouldn't be able reform and assault them again.

Such was Bohemond's stature and the height of his horse that he was one of the first to observe the scene of Rainald and his men driving the enemy backwards. Routing them. Others may have doubted the small miracle they were witnessing, or thought they were suffering from heatstroke, but the Norman always believed that it didn't have to wholly be a defensive battle. They could take the fight to their opponents. Victory could happen. Would happen.

Bohemond bellowed over the unholy din and instructed a nearby officer to signal new orders. Trumpets were sounded. Flags raised. Godfrey of Bouillon didn't need to be told twice. He asked an attendant to load his crossbow and addressed his troops.

"Draw your weapons. Fight for God. Fight for your loved ones in the city. Fight for your Christian brethren marching alongside you. But fight. Kill the infidel, else they will kill you," Godfrey proclaimed to his loyal soldiers, before briefly closing his eyes to offer up a private prayer to God, to keep his countrymen safe.

Whispers sounded above or below the chink of mail and clang of plate armour. Word was spreading that Rainald of Toul had beaten the enemy back. God was on their side. Many pilgrims took heart from Raymond of Aguilers, carrying the Holy Lance, advancing (Adhemar, though no worshipper of the relic, was still wise enough to devote some of his mounted troops to guard the chaplain).

"Stay behind me lad when the fun begins – but make sure you stick anyone who looks like they might stick me," Edward said, his features hardening, like cement setting, as he marched forward.

Robert of Flanders plucked a few arrows out of his shield and tapped the flank of his warhorse, to advance. He was pleasantly surprised by the lack of momentum the enemy were displaying in moving forward. Despite their numbers, reaching back across the plains, the pilgrim armies needed only to engage and defeat the front ranks. And then the next front ranks. They would not be able to bring their multitudes to bear.

"I can smell their fear men, as surely as you can smell shit in a stable. Let's give them a taste of their own medicine. Archers, nock your arrows. Let's show these heathens how to properly shoot a bow. It'll be the last lesson they ever learn. Pull. Imagine you're poaching again. It's time to go hunt and kill. Loose!"

The swoosh of arrows was accompanied by roars of exertion and satisfaction, as the bowmen arced their arrows over the men-at-arms in front of them and into the enemy, many of whom hadn't raised their shields properly to protect themselves. The force of the volley was deadly, far deadlier than the efforts of their opponents. The archers had protected their bowstrings from the rain. Owen had advised his men to "keep it under your hat" – and his words were passed on.

Tancred mobilised his forces too, positioning his cavalry to the rear of his row of infantry. The plan was for his men-at-arms to punch a hole into the enemy ranks – and for his mounted knights to turn a fissure into a chasm. He would mow his opponents down – slice open their backs as well as their purses. What good was glory without gold too?

Kerbogha's forces at the frontline checked their step a little, their feet hanging in the air a moment longer than necessary, when they saw the enemy advancing. Some, including emirs, had stared across the plains, through the rain and dusty haze, and absorbed the sight of Asim's army retreating. Were the Christians carrying the Holy Lance, as rumoured? Was the divine weapon real? Concern etched itself into the burnished, fleshy features of many of the emirs. Kerbogha had underestimated the pilgrims – and exacerbated his folly through further poor decisions. He should have attacked the enemy immediately, as soon as they left the city, instead of letting the infidels choose their terrain. He should have sent a greater force and a more experienced commander to engage their left flank. Petty vanity had prevented him from allowing Marwan to storm the city. He had frequently called the westerners "easy prey" and "dead men walking". Allah was punishing him for his pride. A large faction of emirs had spoken beforehand about betraying their power-hungry commander. Allah willed it. The Prophet would approve. Why should they sacrifice their armies to help a mere atabeg, with ideas above his station, to gain sway over them? The pilgrims had no place to retreat to and would fight to the death. The price of giving battle would be high. Too high.

The Emirs of Homs and Aleppo sat on their fine horses and gazed across at each other. They were sufficiently close to observe the imperious nod they gave one another – and be the first to give the order for their troops to withdraw.

The rain had caused the ground to soften. Mud and blood splattered upwards, as the two sides fought at close quarters. There were few stances and strokes that Edward employed which could be found in the illustrated books Thomas had read on swordsmanship. The English knight smashed a gauntleted fist into the terrified face of a Turkish warrior, as he lay on a bed of corpses. At the same time Edward slashed his blade upwards and sliced open an opponent's lips and crooked nose. Thomas stood just to the side and behind his countryman, jabbing his sword forward when he could. Courage (or self-preservation) was, just about, getting the better of his cowardice. He repeatedly recalled Owen's instructions, like he was a pupil conjugating Latin verbs again. "Aim for the groin, neck, face."

Other knights similarly slashed away, with more ferocity than finesse, along the line. Thomas could hear Fulk of Chartres' booming voice over the tumultuous melee. He cursed his enemies and berated his own troops to advance quicker as he swung his bloody axe - kicking, butting and even biting those he engaged. The knight had been the first crusader to scale the ladder when infiltrating Antioch a month before.

He was keen to be the first to break through the enemy lines now.

More horns, more orders, blared out from the rear of the Muslim ranks – but they were distinctly different from those which had come before. Thomas understood the orders he was hearing being yelled out – but it took him a moment to believe his eyes and ears. Turks and Arabs, Sunni and Shia, alike withdrew – far quicker than they advanced. For once they were displaying unity.

Others from behind rushed by him but Edward caught his breath and leaned on his sword, like a crutch. Resistance was melting away across the entire battlefield. Most Turks were now retreating, regardless of hearing any orders. The knight strangely and sublimely recalled an episode in a village just outside of Rheims, between campaigns. It was winter. Snowing. It was bitterly cold even at midday – and the soldier was bitterly sober. He attempted to enter the local tavern but the bolts to the door had been frozen shut. He was tempted to smash the door open, but the landlord wouldn't be best pleased. Undeterred, Edward tramped through the snow to the neighbouring church and returned, carrying a several lighted candle. For once candles can be put to good use, he thought to himself. They're at least answering my prayers. The flames thawed out the ice. Edward fleetingly mused to himself how he had never been so happy to see something melt away, until now.

"We did it. We've won. It's over," Thomas said, his face mottled with blood and dirt. Despite the flies buzzing over the open wounds of the dead and dying, despite a festering stench entering his nostrils, he was exultant. The scribe might have wept, if he wasn't so exhausted. Other pilgrims emitted breathless cheers or fell to their knees, giving thanks to God.

"Not yet," Edward replied, as he eyed the flags on top of Kerbogha's tent.

20.

Whether from bloodlust - or knowing that a dead army was preferable to a defeated one which could reform and return to give battle - the crusaders were not content with the Turks just withdrawing. The princes and their companies of mounted knights led the charge, like hounds pursuing a fox.

Godfrey of Bouillon didn't want to waste the hours of practise time he had spent shooting his crossbow at full gallop. Bohemond ordered his cavalry to wound as many of the enemy as possible – and move onto their next prey. "Just hobble them. Our infantry can finish them off." Tancred ordered his men to hunt in packs, as he hawkishly targeted those wearing expensive armour or riding fine mounts. Even Count Hartmann of Dillengen dug his spurs into his donkey, to move faster and keep him at the vanguard of the action.

Such was the chaotic extent of the rout that the first wave of Turkish forces crashed into the second, led by Kerbogha, whose troops were supposed to finish off any opposition. Soldiers were knocked down and trampled upon in the mud, by horses or their Muslim brothers. It was a form of carnage, without anyone employing their weapons. The second wave soon retreated in the direction of the first, unable to swim against the stream. The tide was going out, not in. Kerbogha initially remained mute, like a man helplessly watching his house burn down. But then he raged like a fire, threatening to execute anyone who deserted. But there were now far more deserters than loyal troops. There was no threat, or bribe, he could offer to compel his men to fight instead of flee. Even members of his personal retinue and bodyguard were scattering in the wind, like blossom falling from a tree.

"We are a grand army, a mountain that cannot be moved," he bawled, contrary to events and his thoughts.

Janus! Scorpions! May Allah strike you and your seed down. The Prophet sees all. Imams will hear of your treachery and slit your throats while you pray.

"Radwan! Radwan!" Kerbogha called, swivelling his head, his voice breaking with the strain. He wanted his lieutenant close, to guard him and plan his next move. The commander didn't believe it was checkmate quite yet. But Radwan had peeled away, ordering a handful of other mounted troops to follow him – having spotted his prey of the English knight across the battlefield.

After catching his breath and taking stock Edward issued a few orders to the soldiers around him. He sought out the men Bohemond had put under his command, including Thomas. Before the battle Edward had decided that his mission to try to infiltrate Kerbogha's tent would be too perilous. There would be an army between him and his target. But that was then. The impossible had suddenly become probable. Enemy soldiers were scattering like insects. A path for him had been cleared, like Moses parting the waters. Edward thought of Emma. If he could secure even part of Kerbogha's treasury for Bohemond, then neither of them would have to toil again. He could purchase a house and a share in a tavern, back in England. His dream could be realised. Miracles can happen, as evidenced by the reversal of fortune today, he considered.

The scene before the knight was fractured and bloody. The camp was still some way off. The enemy hadn't been completely vanquished. Screams still splintered the air, causing some to wince as if they were chewing on shards of glass. Edward gazed to his left and was attracted to the sight of Adhemar leading a cavalry charge. Thankfully, the men Bohemond had paid to protect the bishop were sticking to him like Myrmidons. The butcher's bill would indeed be high if Adhemar's name was listed on it. Bohemond knew that the princes would be united in grief for a week if the bishop died, but then they might be united against him, or all turn on each other, soon afterwards. Adhemar knew it too, having confided in the English knight.

"I feel like Cicero sometimes, trying to keep our body politic together. Unfortunately, Bohemond and Raymond are all too willing to behave like Caesar and Pompey."

Adhemar would survive his current engagement. Watching him use a sword and control his warhorse, it was difficult to believe that the skilled warrior was also a priest. The knight sometimes found it difficult to believe that other men were priests too, albeit for different reasons.

There was plenty happening around him for Edward's attention to be pulled away from worrying about his friend. Christians were slitting throats, cutting off ears to secure jewellery. Some Muslims raised their hands in surrender or dropped to their knees to beg for mercy and be taken prisoners – but the pilgrims knew there was not enough food to go around to feed themselves, let alone others. The victors also recalled the misery and starvation they had endured whilst being besieged – and the grief over the death of loved ones. Clemency seemed unnatural, wrong – the last thing on their mind.

Thomas cringed and nearly vomited upon witnessing a man-at-arms cleave open a Turk's skull with a forester's axe, shouting obscenities at his foe as if he were still alive. The scribe also took in a confrontation between a knight and enemy archer. The Muslim spat in the knight's face. In return the Frank drew a bodkin and plunged it into the Arab's eye – before spitting on the dead body. Thomas couldn't help but conclude however that it was the newly recruited pilgrims, signing up to fight after the discovery of the lance, who proved the most zealous in their cruelty. Murder was no longer a mortal sin. It was more akin to a reward. They hunted in groups, torturing and tormenting any wounded they could find. Their hands crawled over bodies, like lice, searching for any scraps of food. They believed they were instruments of God – and divine justice – even when they placed their fingers up a corpse's posterior to check if there were any valuables concealed there. Thomas didn't question whether chivalry was dead. He wondered if it had ever existed in the first place.

Edward could see in the distance that the area surrounding Kerbogha's settlement of tents was still populous with enemy troops. He wondered whether their general had ordered his men to secure his treasury or valuables, or if his own soldiers were looting from him. The numbers seemed to be thinning, however, as swathes of crusaders were approaching. Edward was confident that he could cut his way through the cordon and make his fortune.

But the knight would never reach the cluster of tents. The dream was over, sucked into a void, as Edward witnessed Radwan riding at the tip of a spearhead of mounted troops. Riding towards him. Both the hulking infidel and his horse widened their nostrils and snorted. Although no great believer in fate, the Englishman thought he would encounter the Muslim at some point during the battle. Edward looked around for a contingent of cavalry to all upon, to intercept the enemy, but to no avail. He and his men appeared stranded. Radwan held his scimitar aloft, as if wanting to show his enemy the weapon he would slay him with.

The westerner would pay for his insolence and blasphemy, from their previous confrontation. If there was time, he would hack off the filthy heathen's head and present it to his master as a trophy. It would be of little consolation at the end of such a devastating day, but it might be a start. They might still have the numbers to rebuild their grand army. Radwan would deal with the treacherous emirs personally, if asked to. Nothing but their deaths should answer for their dishonour. The battle might be lost, but the war wasn't over, he vowed to Allah.

The band of soldiers accompanying Edward remained temporarily startled, like deer caught in the gaze of a group of poachers with arrows resting on their bows. They didn't have the time and numbers to form into a defensive square, with spears sticking out like porcupine needles, to fend off the attack. If they attempted to run off in different directions, they would be easily picked off too.

"With me, men," Edward announced, as he led the withdrawal back towards their own lines. None thought they would make it, however. The race would be akin to a contest between a hare and tortoise. The glutinous mud made it seem to Edward like he was tramping through the snow again. Many of the pilgrims kept turning around, to take in the ever-encroaching horsemen - their lances set in position to skewer their quarry. At some point the crusaders would attempt to fend off the attack. But it would be in vain.

The thrum of the galloping horses beat as fast as his heart. The ground shook, worse than before, Thomas thought. He felt his legs might buckle, from fear or fatigue. He began to pray. Thomas hoped that if he perished mid-prayer then his soul might be delivered.

"The tall knight is mine," Radwan barked, over the tamp of hooves churning up the ground. None of the horsemen would dare disobey the infamous officer. A slither of drool ran down the Muslim's chin, perhaps due to salivating over devouring his prey.

The Turks grew so close that they commenced their ululating war cries.

Edward retreated.

But it was a feigned retreat. A trap. He had arranged with Owen beforehand for his group of archers to shadow him during the advance towards Kerbogha's tent. The Welshman rightly judged that the figure at the head of the cavalry charge was the same bastard who had slaughtered Hugh de Cerisy. He pulled his bowstring back a little further, in honour of the dead knight. The arrow punched through Radwan's cuirass as if it wasn't there. The brawny warrior slowly fell from his horse, as if had fallen asleep, and was briefly dragged along the ground from his right foot being trapped in the stirrup. Owen's arrow was the first of many, as his fellow archers let loose a swarm of missiles into the enemy horsemen. "I want their heads to resemble pin cushions," the Welshman had remarked, as they readied their bows. Some of the Turks were knocked backwards off their horses, from the force of the arrows. With the head of the snake cut off, the fight went out of the remaining soldiers immediately. They didn't need to be ordered to abandon the attack and retreat. Desert. Edward was able to draw his dagger and launch it into the back of a Turk as he attempted to wheel his horse around.

Thomas, still a little shaken, was not alone in offering up a prayer of thanks for being alive. He also thanked God for Herleva.

Edward, with no small effort, kicked over Radwan's corpse to see his face mangled, caked in mud and blood. He felt a fleeting, almost religious, wave of satisfaction. But then he felt next to nothing. Edward's only regret was that the fiend's death had been too quick, too merciful. The knight had wanted to look his foe in the eye, before he died. Part of the soldier also wanted to test himself against the skilled Muslim, to succeed where Conrad had failed. Had he acted in a slightly dishonourable way, vanquishing his enemy in such an unchivalrous manner? But part of him, more of him, wanted to just return safely to Emma. Being dishonourable was preferable to being dead, the knight coldly concluded.

Edward told his men to stand down, after they duly thanked the bowmen for their timely intervention. They deserved a respite from the pandemonium unfurling, like victory banners, around them. He decided that they would not recommence their attack on the enemy camp. One near death experience was enough for the day. Instead, the Englishman clasped hands with his Welsh companion.

"It seems like you owe me your life, again," Owen said, his grin resembling the shape of his bow.

"Will you accept sharing a jug of wine, instead?"

"By God, yes."

21.

Epilogue.

Kerbogha and the remnants of his army were routed. Many Syrians and Armenians in the region slaughtered swathes of deserters as they dispersed and tried to make their way back home. Kerbogha the Dreadful now earned the title of Kerbogha the Defeated. In one way the commander had achieved his ambition of making a name for himself. History would remember him, but not in the way he wished for. The general had plenty of time to make a list of those who were to blame for his grand army's ignominious defeat, although his own name on it was conspicuous by its absence.

The pilgrims awarded their miraculous triumph to God. Plenty of crusaders attested to seeing visions of various saints, riding on white horses, join them in the fighting. Others swore they witnessed that the enemy commander was rendered mute, upon observing the Holy Lance.

Ahmad Marwan, realising which way the wind had blown, initiated the surrender of the citadel. Raymond of Toulouse was only too pleased to hear the news and take possession of the asset. Marwan decreed, however, that he would only surrender the stronghold to Bohemond of Taranto. The Norman had sent a message to the commander before the battle that, should the pilgrims prove victorious, he would agree safe passage for the Muslim and his garrison. On the condition that Marwan surrendered the citadel to him personally. He declined the opportunity to make his way own back home. Believing Bohemond to now be the preeminent magnate in the region, Marwan converted to Christianity and joined the Norman's company. Raymond again felt like he had come second in a jousting competition.

After the battle, Bohemond rewarded Edward with a large jug of wine. The satisfaction and relief experienced by the prince eclipsed any disappointment he felt at the Englishman's failure at completing his mission.

"You fought well, Edward, but I expected nothing else... I have heard numerous reports earlier that St George fought well beside us too... Know that whenever we line up to give battle again, I would still prefer to see you standing next to me than any saint or angel, not least because I couldn't afford the rates of pay for the latter."

Edward ventured home and duly started working his way through the wine, with Emma. After a few barely diluted measures the knight finally mustered the courage to ask his companion to marry him.

"Has this been the reason for the wine, to make me more compliant and biddable?" Emma remarked, smiling into her cup.

"Aye. I know that no woman in their right mind would want to marry me sober."

"Just as long as I can get married in white. It'll amuse me to scandalise any onlookers."

Adhemar declined the invitation, citing ill-health, to lead a celebratory mass after the victory, with the Holy Lance taking pride of place. Peter Bartholomew was only too glad to stand in for the bishop. Raymond of Toulouse made a miracle recovery and rose from his deathbed to address the congregation, whilst holding the relic.

A rival mass was delivered by Peter the Hermit in a market square, although he couldn't help but note that his flock had been shorn of numbers. In a barely concealed reference to his namesake, he warned his congregants to "Beware of false prophets," without the merest hint of irony or shame.

Thomas was keen to avoid both services. He was compelled to visit the Church of St Jude, however, before meeting with Herleva. He rightly predicted that the chapel would be quiet. He wanted to hear his own thoughts, find some peace and piety. Although the pilgrim couldn't claim to be endowed with the same strength or strain of faith he owned when he had set off on the campaign, a fog had lifted from his mind. God was no longer an enemy, or absent. Thomas unfastened his sword and kneeled down to pray. He could recall once more his favourite psalms and verses from the Bible.

The Lord's unfailing love and mercy still continue,
Fresh as the morning, as sure as the sunrise.
The Lord is all I have, and so I put my hope in him.

Thomas prayed for God to guide him in his journey, to show him a sign as to what he should do next. Should he march on to Jerusalem, or back to England? Thomas also prayed for his parents, Herleva and Edward. He prayed that Emma would assent to his friend's marriage proposal. Before Antioch, the Christian would have blanched at the notion of someone marrying a "jezebel". But now Thomas was happy for his friend. God moves in mysterious ways. Love can blossom in the strangest of places. He thought of Herleva. *I may have all the faith needed to move mountains – but if I have no love, I am nothing.* Thomas pictured the young woman naked and was understandably prompted to end his prayers and seek her out.

As Thomas was leaving the church, he encountered a figure he had seen there before. Godfrey of Bouillon. Like Thomas, the Christian prince craved some peace and piety. Godfrey needed to prove to himself, as well as others, that he was a man of God as well as a man of war. He also possessed little desire to celebrate mass with a throng of commoners. He intended to pray to God to forgive the sins of his men. Although a contingent of his Lotharingians had resisted raping a group of Muslim women they had found, his soldiers had lanced them in their bellies and throats. Godfrey was willing to forgive his men for their overexuberance. He hoped God could do the same. The prince would give due thanks to the Almighty too, for sparing him during the battle. Now, more than ever, Godfrey ardently believed that the crusade was destined to capture Jerusalem – and he would live to see his banner flying over the St Stephen's Gate.

I have been chosen. God wills it.

"You are Thomas, are you not? The Englishman? You fought well today, as did many others," Godfrey equitably remarked.

Thomas thought him every inch a Christian prince. Herleva had once mentioned that she thought Godfrey one of the handsomest men on the campaign. She was right. The prince eclipsed the scrawny scribe in so many ways that Thomas didn't feel a mote of envy towards the nobleman. His countenance was an alloy of strength and nobility. Despite the long and bloody day, the soldier still appeared as though he could ride out again and give battle within the hour.

Thomas nodded, a little overawed, as the words he wished to reply with were stuck in the back of his throat.

"You are a knight?"

"No."

"You should be."

The youth's heart swelled with a goodly sense of pride. His eyes gleamed as brightly as the candles flanking the altar. It was as if God had shown him a sign. Godfrey was aware that Thomas was a mere scribe, but it would do no harm to compliment him – and even offer the pilgrim the opportunity to become a knight. The prince would then have a greater chance of recruiting his friend and countryman, Edward, to his company. Godfrey was in need of a new lieutenant to replace Conrad.

The battle for Antioch was over. But the battle for Jerusalem had yet to begin.

End Note.

Besieged is a work of fiction, but it is based on history. The events leading up to and including the Battle of Antioch are some of the most dramatic in the entire story of the First Crusade. Should you be interested in reading more about the real history behind *Besieged* then I can recommend the following. *The First Crusade*, by Thomas Asbridge. *A History of the Crusades: The First Crusade*, by Steven Runciman.

Please do get in touch should you have enjoyed *Besieged*, or any of my other novels. It's always nice – and useful – to receive feedback from readers. Thank you to all those people who have recently been in contact about my first medieval series, *Band of Brothers*, and the *Spies of Rome* novels. Similarly, I am grateful to all those readers who emailed me in relation to *Siege*. I dare say your comments and encouragement helped to shape *Besieged*. I can be contacted via richard@sharpebooks or @rforemanauthor on Twitter.

Edward Kemp and Thomas Devin will return in *Jerusalem*.

Richard Foreman

Printed in Great Britain
by Amazon